The Wit and Wisdom of The NORTH

The Wit and Wisdom of The NORTH

ROSEMARIE JARSKI

EBURY
PRESS

1 3 5 7 9 10 8 6 4 2

First published in 2009 by Ebury Press, an imprint of Ebury Publishing

A Random House Group company

The Random House Group Limited Reg. No. 954009

Addresses for companies within the Random House Group can be found at www.randomhouse.co.uk

A CIP catalogue record for this book is available from the British Library

The Random House Group Limited supports The Forest Stewardship Council (FSC), the leading international forest certification organisation. All our titles that are printed on Greenpeace approved FSC certified paper carry the FSC logo. Our paper procurement policy can be found at www.rbooks.co.uk/environment

Mixed Sources

Product group from well-managed forests and other controlled sources
www.fsc.org Cert no. TT-COC-2139
© 1996 Forest Stewardship Council

FSC

Printed in the UK by CPI Mackays, Chatham, ME5 8TD

ISBN 9780091932336

To buy books by your favourite authors and register for offers visit www.rbooks.co.uk

The moral applies to the whole Kingdom of the North: 'Never ask a man if he comes from Yorkshire. If he does, he will tell you without asking. If he does not, why humiliate him?'

Roy Hattersley

To Mum and Milena – Galapagos turtles both

Contents

PLACES

RELATIONSHIPS AND FAMILY LIFE

SPORT AND RECREATION

THE NATURAL WORLD

ARTS AND ENTERTAINMENT

POLITICS AND SOCIETY

SCIENCE AND TECHNOLOGY

BODY, MIND AND SOUL

LIFE, THE UNIVERSE AND EVERYTHING ELSE

Foreword

by Stuart Maconie

To misquote L.P. Hartley, 'The North is a foreign country, they do things differently there'. I expect the Bistro-ites of Islington and Brighton imagine that we do it in pelts and woad under lead grey skies whilst dying of diphtheria.

But no. While there is a strain of the northern psyche and imagination that is dark and mordant and brooding, we are also whimsical and romantic. We are elegiac and thoughtful. We are, above all, a right laugh – as I hope you will soon see.

Here you will find you are in the very best of company with some of the finest minds of this or any other generation; Morrissey, Alan Bennett, Jarvis Cocker, Victoria Wood, Mark E. Smith, Jeanette Winterson, Peter Tinniswood and more. Natural modesty forbids me from mentioning – oh, go on then – that there is even a nugget or two from myself in here, chiefly on matters of the gravest import such as chippies, Northern soul music and the Lancastrian fondness for the pastry savoury.

This is a book full of wry observation, thought-provoking insights and outright hilarity. Spending an hour or two in its company is bracing and educational. I myself learned many things and none more strange and wonderful than the fact that, according to Anthony Burgess, Graham Greene put carrots in his Lancashire hotpot. Burgess seems to have thought this an aberration but I consider it completely acceptable, *de rigeur* even.

And I like to think of our greatest novelist of Catholic guilt and forbidden sexual desire standing at the sink in an apron, dicing merrily, while the Bisto thickens on the stove.

Introduction

—Tell me, Eric, what would you and Ernie have been if you weren't comedians?
—Mike and Bernie Winters.

Interviewer and Eric Morecambe

Hello playmates!

It's thrilling to be invited to compile *The Wit and Wisdom of The North* not least because you know you're in for a lorra lorra laughs, but even a labour of love is not without its challenges. Northern Pride is at stake. You want to do justice to our rich comic heritage. You want to show us at our best. Let's be honest: you want to show those soft southern jessies who really rules the country when it comes to humour. To succeed, tough decisions must to be taken and important ground rules laid down.

First, define your territory. 'The North' is a movable feast, depending on your location, so an imaginary dividing line has to be drawn somewhere. I took the plunge in the River Trent (very bracing, lucky I took a towel), nominating Stoke-on-Trent as the official tollgate where vowels and caps start to flatten. Rest assured, the choice was determined by strict socio-geographical imperatives, taking into consideration historical and topographical boundaries dating back to William the Conqueror, and had absolutely nothing to do with the fact that I have a cracking Robbie Williams quote. Honest.

Next, define your Northerner. Silly me thought it would simply be a matter of invoking the old Yorkshire cricket team selection process and saying, 'If you were born in the North, you're a Northerner.' Which is fine till you discover that Caroline Aherne was born in London and John Prescott was born in Prestatyn, and how can you have a collection of Northern humour without two of its best comedians? Oh, for the days when all you had to do was spot somebody with mutton-chop whiskers, a pot-belly and a ferret down their trousers. (And it was just as easy to identify the men.)

If only there was a foolproof method of testing for a real Northerner, as there is for a real princess in the Hans Christian Andersen fairy story: Slip a mushy pea under their Slumberland and check next morning what sort of a night's sleep they had. 'Appen we could enquire if they prefer Tetley's or Earl Grey; say 'laff' or 'larf'; have meat pie crumbs round their mouth; support Manchester United (which, obviously would prove they're southern). A friend had a theory: 'Everyone in the North thinks Birmingham is in the South; everyone in the South thinks Birmingham is in the North.' First person I asked, 'Where's Birmingham?' replied, 'It's in the Midlands.'

Up the Mersey without a tickling stick, I asked myself the question I always ask in times of trouble: What would Ken Dodd do? 'By Jove, missus!' the Squire of Knotty Ash would say. 'Don't get discomknockerated! Open a jar of good old-fashioned Northern nous and apply liberally to the affected area.' So I did, and before you could say, 'tattifilarious', I had my ruling: If I say they're Northern, they're bloody well Northern and that's that. Like it or lump it.

If I inadvertently ascribe Northern nationality to any non-nationals, I apologise (blame Doddy), but trust they will accept the compliment in good grace and consider themselves honorary citizens at least between the covers of this volume.

Finally, define Northern humour. Give over! You're having a laugh! How do you define a reflex, something that comes to us as naturally as drinking, I mean, blinking. In the North, a sense of humour is bred in the (funny) bone, hardwired into our folk DNA, and, as such, taken for granted. In fact, you only appreciate how special our humour is and how blessed we are to have it if you're lucky enough to be engaged on a project like this – or unlucky enough to cross the border.

Northern humour is, above all, the humour of recognition. Northern comedians don't try to be cleverer or smarter than us, they're inclusive rather than exclusive. Southern comics tell us how they got one over on someone; Northern comics tell us what a prat they made of themselves. There are no airs and graces, no attempts at one-upmanship. They're one of us.

But don't take my word for it. Dave Spikey, who's at the coalface of comedy, explains the differences:

My act is very northern... You get these comedians trying to be really right on and topical and they're all technically brilliant. And then I'll come on at the end and go, 'Ruddy Wigan, eh?' and the people all go, 'Whooahh, that's what we want, a bit of that!' There's a difference with northern comics. On stage it's like we're having a chat. With others you just get material, none of them in it.

What Dave Spikey has is that simple but elusive quality: warmth. Like charisma, it can't be bought, it can't be taught, but, by 'eck, it oozes from the pores of Northern comics like curry fumes after a takeaway vindaloo. Think of Les Dawson, Morecambe and Wise, Peter Kay, Johnny Vegas, Jason Manford, Jeff Green, Lee Mack, John Bishop, Ross Noble (how long d'you have?). We connect with these characters on an emotional level, making for a deeper, richer and, ultimately, funnier experience.

Sure, it's a cliché, but the big-hearted and friendly disposition of our comedians reflects the general nature of this part of the world, where people still talk to you at bus stops. ('Give us yer fuckin' mobile or I'll fuckin' deck yer!' is what they usually say, but, hey, you can't have everything.) Warmth is also built into the accent. 'If Father Christmas were to speak, he'd have a Northern accent – cosy, big and heartfelt,' according to Jenny Eclair. The Northern accent is easier on the ear than cockney, and more amenable to southern ears. Critic James Christopher described the voice of Wallace (Peter Sallis) in 'Wallace and Gromit' as 'a warm pair of slippers in an uncertain world'. Reassuring and reliable. J.B. Priestley reckoned that listening to the original Lancashire lass, Gracie Fields, for just fifteen minutes would tell you more about Lancashire women and Lancashire than a dozen books on the subjects. 'All the qualities are there,' he asserted, 'shrewdness, homely simplicity, irony, fierce independence, an impish delight in mocking whatever is thought to be affected and pretentious.' That goes for the rest of the North too.

A keen ear for dialogue is essential in the comedy of recognition, and one humorist supremely skilled at capturing the peculiar rhythms of Northern speech was Peter Tinniswood. He was born in Liverpool, but grew up in Sale in Greater Manchester where he lived with his mum above a dry-cleaner's. He used to sit under the counter among the dirty laundry and eavesdrop on the conversations in the shop. 'It was like live radio,' he explained. 'It sharpened my ear for dialogue...I became a good mimic.'

What makes the dialogue of Peter Tinniswood so resonant is an authenticity borne of the writer's deep identification with his homeland. The poet, Roy Fisher, has said of his own birthplace in the Midlands, 'Birmingham's what I think with'. The North's what Peter Tinniswood thought with. And he was passionate about it. That love found its greatest expression in the character of Uncle Mort, the dour, lugubrious hero of a series of novels, who was brought memorably to life by Robin Bailey in the television series, *I Didn't Know You Cared*.

As a comic creation, Uncle Mort eclipses Basil Fawlty, Del Boy Trotter and Norman Stanley Fletcher, and ranks alongside Falstaff, Mr Pickwick and Homer Simpson. Who else owns an allotment on which he cultivates only weeds and hoists a flag whenever he is in residence? Who else asks questions like, 'Do you think the Holy Ghost could play for Yorkshire if it could be proved he were born in Sheffield?' And who else, given the news he has cancer, says to his brother-in-law, on their way to the pub, 'Don't mention owt about my impending fatality. I don't want no one thinking I'm trying to be a bloody show-off.'

Uncle Mort is the living embodiment of the North: 'His mind is a rag-bag of folk memories and lovingly nurtured prejudices, and from his unstoppable mouth flows a kind of comic version of the North's collective unconscious,' writes critic Glyn Turton. Mort belonged to the generation that created the popular idea of the North. They were proper heroes who suffered privations we cannot begin to imagine and fought two world wars to give us the freedom we now take for granted. Uncle Mort's beloved open-top trams, condensed milk sandwiches and cloth cap may now be sacred relics consigned to the mythology of the North, but his spirit lives on: grit, guts, gumption and grumpiness – all that's grand about the Northern character.

Mort is timeless, but also of his time, espousing views that would make Germaine Greer turn in her grave – if she were dead. For example, his idea of t'perfect woman is 'a bloke with big knockers' and he can only countenance a Heaven that is 'men-only'. Sexism is an accusation regularly levelled at the humour of the North and, as home to Andy Capp, Roy 'Chubby' Brown and *Viz* magazine, it's a tough charge to defend. You might argue, these mirth-makers are merely mirroring reality: the North is still a stronghold of the Unreconstructed Male. Metrosexuals have yet to catch on in Barnsley. Male moisturiser does not fly off the shelves of Superdrug in Scunthorpe. And any battle of the sexes is, by definition, going to be sexist. If all the material that might be deemed politically incorrect had been censored, this would have been a shorter, duller and less truthful book. Judgements were made in accordance with regulations laid down by Graham Dury, the *Viz* cartoonist who invented 'The Fat Slags': 'We never like upsetting people. If something goes in, it's got to be funnier than it is offensive.'

One comedian unjustly tarred with the 'sexist' brush was Les Dawson. As king of the mother-in-law joke, he caught the full force of the Feminist onslaught. But he put up a cogent and compelling defence (and still managed to slip a few gags in):

Surely no one could take my remarks seriously. When I say my mother-in-law is a decoy for whaling ships, that her skin is stretched so tightly that when she bends her knees her eyelids fly open, I mean, come on... It's cartoon imagery. It's a lampoon. It's basically affection, anyway. I don't pull anything to pieces that I don't like. Things I don't like, I ignore. Things I'm fond of, I make fun of.

Les grew up in working-class Collyhurst surround by women, with an 'auntie' on every street. Women were the glue that held communities together. Northern women were a breed apart. Alan Bennett describes their evolution: 'They have come down by a separate genetic route and like the Galapagos turtles (whom some of them resemble) they have developed their own characteristics.' So, what might those characteristics be – apart from scaly skin and a rock-hard shell? Stoicism, pragmatism, resilience, self-reliance and resourcefulness – Northern women are born copers. As an Alan Bennett lass puts it: 'I could probably deliver a baby if I was ever called upon and I can administer an enema at a moment's notice.'

And they can deliver a quip and administer a rebuke even faster! Men rarely get the better of women in the Northern war of words; they're outwitted, outsmarted and outfoxed. According to the *London Review of Books*: 'Women do most of the talking in northern plays, men in London-based plays'. The fair sex certainly nab the lion's share of the lines in Northern soap operas. The success and longevity of *Coronation Street* is largely down to the consistently strong female characters who have stalked the cobbles down its long history, from Ena Sharples to Blanche Hunt. By all accounts, Violet Carson, who played Ena, the hair-netted harridan, was just as formidable in real life. She once introduced herself to a new director on set with the words: 'My name is Violet Carson and my train leaves at five o'clock.' The Witches of Weatherfield epitomise what Les Dawson calls the 'doorstep doyennes in bright aprons, arms akimbo as they pass judgement on the neighbourhood morality'. A few more like them on our streets today and we'd soon solve the scourge of the hoodie.

Northern women speak as they find; they have licence to say things their male counterparts couldn't get away with. Which explains (though only in part, mind), why so many male Northern comics can't wait to slip a hairy leg into a pair of lady's fishnets. Steve Coogan's female alter ego is Pauline Calf, displaying pins so shapely that many red-blooded males confess to fancying her/him. Paul O'Grady is the brassy blonde bombsite, Lily Savage. And then there's the unforgettable double act of Roy Barraclough and Les Dawson as Cissie Braithwaite and Ada Shufflebottom.

Les was a consummate pantomime dame and fan of musical-hall star Norman Evans on whose *Over the Garden Wall* character he based Ada. He revelled in the part of the coarse old crone, hoisting his huge prosthetic bosoms in fidgety awkwardness as he discussed his/her problems 'down there' and mouthed the unmentionable words. (Btw – the verb to describe this action is 'mee-maw'. It derives from the exaggerated expressions of workers in the cotton mills to make themselves understood over the noise of the machinery. Even when the cotton mills closed down, the practice continued. You can see it in 'Wallace and Gromit', in the way Wallace enunciates his words with slow and deliberate precision: 'CHEEEEEESE, GROMIT...') Drag acts are still popular today, and the latest incarnations of Cissie and Ada appear on TV's *Loose Women* in the forms of Coleen Nolan and Jane McDonald, though, if you ask me, their prosthetic bosoms are way too big to be convincing.

In a male-dominated field like comedy, it is a rare treat to be able to include so many first-rate female wits. There was no question of filling quotas; admission was entirely on merit. What a bubbling hotpot of Norsewomen, including Jenny Eclair, Caroline Aherne, Nancy Banks-Smith, Beryl Bainbridge, Maureen Lipman, Carla Lane and the jewel in the crown – or should that be the currant in the Chorley cake – Victoria Wood.

Nobody has done more to swell collective pride in our comic tradition than this Prestwich-born comedian and writer. She blazed a trail for female stand-ups after the sadly premature death of Marti Caine from leukaemia ('I'm a lymphomaniac,' she quipped after her diagnosis). Victoria Wood has never played the Northern card; indeed, she resists labelling: 'There are a few professional Northerners about and I'm trying not to be one of them.' In her work, she often pokes fun at the Hovis ad image of the North. But her sensibility is unequivocally Northern, she hasn't lost her amiable Lancastrian tones and she still speaks fondly of her roots. She gives a voice to all middle-aged women who, like older people, are marginalised and ignored by a society obsessed with youth and celebrity. As she grows older, her stand-up routines grow bolder, darker, more up-close and personal – and even funnier.

In common with many Northern wits, Victoria Wood is adept at spinning comic gold out of pain and misery. Laughter and tears are never far apart in Northern Life. Plenty of writers can make you laugh, then make you cry, but only the very best can make you laugh and cry at the same time. Caroline Aherne and Craig Cash regularly wring tears of both laughter and sadness out of their classic slice of Northern working-class life, *The Royle Family* (ably assisted by a sterling cast). In 'The Queen of Sheba', the episode dealing with the death of Nana, comedy and tragedy are held in perfect harmony without ever lapsing into sentimentality. After Nana's funeral, skinflint Jim Royle, who enjoyed a prickly relationship with his mother-in-law, speaks a line that betrays all his latent fondness: 'I'd give all the bloody money in the world to 'ave one more bloody row with 'er.' Hilarious *and* heartbreaking.

The paradoxical propensity to couch affection in abuse is a distinctly Northern trait. 'I think there's a Northern sensibility that involves humour and directness,' says Lee Hall, writer of *Billy Elliot*. 'When you're up north you realise that it's a term of affection to call somebody a bastard.' W.R. Mitchell, renowned former editor of *The Dalesman*, notes a conversation he once heard 'that began with what a stranger would take to be offensive but, in the context of Yorkshire farmers, was affectionate, "Na then, you miserable owd bugger..."' Instead of using players' first names, football manager Brian Clough used to call them, 'Shithouse' – 'it's an affectionate term,' he maintained. And I'm reminded of a bloke approaching Roy 'Chubby' Brown after a show up North, brandishing a programme to be autographed. 'It's for me sister,' he explained. 'Can you put: "To Joanne, you fat cunt".' Ah, there's nowt like sibling love.

What *are* we like? What the holy flamin' hecky plonk must other people make of us? Well, you can pick up a few insights because scattered in amongst the pearls of wit and wisdom from our own kith and kin is the odd gem furnished by offcomers (identified as such by an 'F' for 'Foreigner' – what else? – after their name in the credits). They shine a light on aspects of our character and homeland we ourselves may be too close to pick up on. They also show what bloody good sports we are to be able to take criticism from outside. Chip on our shoulder, us? Nah, more like a full fish-and-chip supper – wi' gravy.

This collection may not bridge the Watford Gap, but any joshing at the expense of our southern cousins is good-natured and laughter-lovers from both sides of the divide are welcomed. Non-Northerners may take a moment or two to acclimatise to the regional voice but familiar themes such as debt, disease and death should make them feel right at home. For, in the end, Northernness is less a matter of geography than it is a state of mind. It's a mindset in which humour plays a crucial if not defining role. So, get a brew on, kick off yer clogs and get stuck in. There hasn't been such glee since the famous lock-in at the Rovers of '76 when it's rumoured Ena Sharples, sozzled on stout, showed Albert Tatlock what she kept under her hairnet. By the 'eck, the pair of 'em staggered out of the snug looking chuffed to little mint balls. As, it's hoped, will you be.

Ay thang yew!

Character

Doorstep Doyennes: **Strong Women**

I came home about two o'clock in the morning on Thursday, and she's stood behind the front door with a rolling pin. I said, 'You're never up at this time baking, are you?'

Roy 'Chubby' Brown

This is God's number-one area for unpleasant women of strong character.

Norman Clegg, *Last of the Summer Wine*

—She were a cold woman, was your Edna. Whenever she was around, it always seemed like the second week in January.
—Aye, that's why I never 'ad much success with me indoor tomatoes.

Les Brandon and Uncle Mort, *I Didn't Know You Cared*

My nan was a very fiery lady, always kicking off... My grandad never got into it...he'd stay silent and tap his foot. And when he got told off for that, he'd go outside and look at his peaches.

Wayne Hemingway

Thelma's mother's arrived. She's wearing that smile of hers – like she's about to unveil the new wing of an abattoir.

Terry Collier, *Whatever Happened to the Likely Lads?*

I once asked my grandma for a biscuit, and she just looked at me and said: 'If we 'ad some 'am, we could 'ave 'am and eggs, but we've no eggs,' and that's me told.

Lucy Mangan (F)

—But, Prime Minister...
—Don't 'but' me, young man...

Margaret Thatcher and Stephen Bayley

Her mouth was like a drawstring bag. You suddenly realised the provenance of the word 'pursed'.

Nancy Banks-Smith

She's that hard faced, if she fell on the pavement she'd crack a flag.

Vera Duckworth, *Coronation Street*

You could fire a bazooka at her and inflict three large holes. Still she kept on coming.

Roy Hattersley, on Margaret Thatcher

I'm what they call in the Hollywood films, 'a dangerous woman'. Barbara Stanwyck could do a picture about me.

Blanche Hunt, *Coronation Street*

—It's only Nora Batty. Despite appearances, she's only human.
—Rubbish. She's legendary.
—If she was in a chariot, you wouldn't be able to move for fleeing Romans!

Seymour Utterthwaite, Wesley Pegden and Norman Clegg,
Last of the Summer Wine

—Go on, make fun of a weak and vulnerable woman.
—I've seen men with balaclavas and sawn-off shotguns more vulnerable than you.

Eileen Grimshaw and Blanche Hunt, *Coronation Street*

Maybe it's because I'm a bolshie-minded Scouser, as my husband would say, that I wanted to stand up for myself.

Cherie Blair

A woman is like a teabag. You never know how strong she is until you put her in hot water.

Natasha Blakeman, *Coronation Street*

Last Of The Summer Whiners: **Grumpiness**

—Nice bloke, that.
—I thought he was very rude – right gruff, right terse, right dour and grumpy.
—That's what I said, nice bloke.

Carter Brandon and Pat Partington, *I Didn't Know You Cared*

To a good West Riding type there is something shameful about praise, that soft Southern trick. But fault-finding and blame are constant and hearty.

J.B. Priestley

I've always been a pessimist. I like the thought of being some kind of depressive drunk, smoking opium like some old poet. That's very appealing.

Michael Parkinson

I have always been a grumbler... Probably I arrived here a malcontent, convinced that I had been sent to the wrong planet... I was designed for the part, for I have a sagging face, a weighty underlip, what I am told is 'a saurian eye', and a rumbling but resonant voice from which it is difficult to escape. Money could not buy a better grumbling outfit.

J.B. Priestley

Women tend to be more personal in their grumping. They tend to react from the gut and the heart, so it's about their home life, their personal looks, their friendships. Men get all huffy and puffy about daft things like football.

Jenny Eclair

He had a tendency to attach far greater significance than was reasonable to the most minor of irritations – light-switches left on, drinks left undrunk, that kind of thing. He also had an absurdly acute sense of smell, which led to a situation whereby we had to leave the house to put on our deodorant.

William, Alexandra, Tom and Florence on their dad, John Peel,
read out at his memorial service

Pessimism, when you get used to it, is just as agreeable as optimism.

Arnold Bennett

I am a life-enhancing pessimist.

J.B. Priestley

No Better Than She Ought To Be: Tarts with Hearts

Here she comes. Catherine of all the bleedin' Russias!

> Tony Warren, greeting a fur-clad Pat Phoenix

Skirt no bigger than a belt, too much eyeliner, and roots as dark as her soul!

> Blanche Hunt, on Liz McDonald, *Coronation Street*

She's twopenn'orth of God-'elp-us wrapped up in a wet 'Echo'.

> Scouse saying

[*Bet is leaning provocatively over the bar*] That Vera. She shoves it all in t'front window, don't she?

> Bet Lynch, *Coronation Street*

Hold yer tongue and put that bosom away when you talk to me, young lady!

> Great Aunt Mona, *I Didn't Know You Cared*

She won't wear anything approaching a brassiere – when she plays ping-pong it puts you in mind of something thought up by Barnes Wallis.

> Kitty, *Victoria Wood, As Seen on TV*

I can't abide women with big busts. In my day, young women didn't 'ave busts; they 'ad modesty. They waited till they was married before they 'ad big busts.

> Great Aunt Mona, *I Didn't Know You Cared*

[*Bet is showing Hilda her low-cut dress*] —By 'eck, it's got a low back 'asn't it?
—That's the front!
—Yer wha'? It's a wonder you don't catch yer death.
—I don't feel cold, Petal. When I wear necklines like that, the temperature round me shoots up to near tropical.

Hilda Ogden and Bet Lynch, Coronation Street

Bet Lynch'll 'ave sequins on her flippin' shroud.

Hilda Ogden, Coronation Street

Somebody else who wears fancier shoes than married feet are entitled to.

Ivy, Last of the Summer Wine

Yana Lumb and Cilla Battersby could lower the tone in a brothel.

Jayne Tunnicliffe, who played Yana Lumb in Coronation Street

Elsie Tanner's a loud-mouthed, pig-'eaded, painted tramp, wi' a bustful o' brassiere an' nowt on top. An' with the right man on 'er arm, she'd turn into the best wife a lad could wish for.

Ena Sharples, Coronation Street

I Want To Live Like Common People: Class Wars and Swanking

I was once on the top of a tram in Leeds with my auntie. We were passing Wellington Road gasworks. She laid a hand on my arm. 'That's the biggest gasworks in England,' she said. 'And I know the manager.'

Alan Bennett

I'm not sayin' she's a bragger, but if *you've* been to Paradise, *she's* got a season ticket... If *you've* got a headache, *she's* got a brain tumour.

Shirley Valentine, *Shirley Valentine*

Annie Walker – she's all lace-curtain accent and brown bread with bits in.

Hilda Ogden, *Coronation Street*

She was so stuck up, she thought her backside was a perfume factory.

Terry Collier, *Whatever Happened to the Likely Lads?*

You don't have to do that to me, my dear – I'm only in politics.

Margaret Thatcher, to a curtseying shop assistant

Margaret Thatcher is democratic enough to talk down to anyone.

Austin Mitchell

My family knew its station all right – we weren't higher than the angels but we were up there with the vicar and the doctor and the schoolmaster. Why else was I dispatched to the chip-shop only after it had grown dark, a pudding basin in a basket on the handlebars of my bike?

Beryl Bainbridge, *Forever England*

I came from a family who had fruit on the sideboard even when no one was ill.

Ted Ray

Grandfather says that until you married mummy, the nearest you came to high society was the Rochdale Mountaineering Club.

Morris Hardacre, *Brass*

7

Just look around, Vera. You've got a nice house, nice furniture, good food on the table, nice bar, nice pictures, loft full o' pigeons, Vauxhall Nova – who could think *we* were common?

Jack Duckworth, *Coronation Street*

His idea of sophistication is a pint of Newcastle Brown with a cherry in it.

Bob Ferris, *Whatever Happened to the Likely Lads?*

—I would say you're working class.
—But I don't work!

John Prescott and Josie Hall (F)

I'm proud to be a chav, if by chav you mean working-class made good.

Cheryl Cole

I'm proud of my home and my class. Just because you're flirting with the lower lower middle middles; just cos you've got yourself an office job and your fiancée lives in a Tudor estate with a monkey puzzle tree…

Terry Collier, *Whatever Happened to the Likely Lads?*

I live in Lytham St Annes where it's so posh that when we eat cod and chips we wear a yachting cap.

Les Dawson

The nice thing about living in Gloucestershire is that none of us have our curtains made by people who haven't got a title.

Anne Robinson

Nigel Havers is surprisingly testy for a man with tassels on his cushions.

Nancy Banks-Smith

The working class and the real upper class have a lot in common. They know where they're from, they like a drink, have a sense of humour. It's the middle you need to look out for.

Mark E. Smith, *Renegade*

Only last week I was at my children's sports day, and as I lay in the long grass by the river drinking pink champagne and chatting with other media parents, I remember thinking, 'I love being middle class.'

Jeremy Clarkson

I knew I'd become middle class when I found myself having an out-of-body experience in Sainsbury's. I looked down on myself and found myself buying a scented candle and a packet of couscous.

Alun Cochrane

I have little or no time for people who aspire to be members of the middle class.

Arthur Scargill

I have news for you, Arthur Scargill. Most working class people wouldn't use a word like 'aspire'. What we do want is your income and lifestyle. What's wrong with that?

Tony Grantham

All the world over I will back the masses against the classes.

William Ewart Gladstone

It's Prim Up North: Manners and Etiquette

It's Mr Clough to you.

Brian Clough, to anyone he didn't know calling him Brian

Call me Brian.

Brian Clough, to anyone he didn't know calling him Mr Clough

They say good manners cost nothing. Bollocks. I sent my daughter to a posh finishing school in Switzerland, and it cost me twenty bastard grand.

Top tip, *Viz* magazine

—How did you bring her up?
—As a lady.
—Then she's handicapped for life. But I've seen some grow out of it.

Miss Metherall and Edmund Whitworth, *The Game*

My kids have beautiful manners. Our Jason may be a car thief but he always leaves a thank you note on the pavement.

Lily Savage, aka Paul O'Grady

My mum did have standards, and although her dad drank his tea out of the saucer, it was not something that was encouraged in her own home.

Alan Titchmarsh, *Nobbut a Lad*

There's one golden rule of etiquette: always tilt the plate towards you when you lick it.

Andy Capp

As Mrs Cannibal said, 'Don't speak with someone in your mouth.'

Mike Harding, *The Armchair Anarchist's Almanac*

Always behave as if nothing had happened, no matter what has happened.

Arnold Bennett

Mardy Bum: Sadness

What's up with you? You've got a face as long as the Mersey Docks and Harbour Board signpost.

Eddie Yates, *Coronation Street*

Come on, stop all these tears. You know it warps the pelmets.

Les Brandon, *I Didn't Know You Cared*

My ferret smiles more than Wally Batty. Mark you, it's got summat to smile about – I use it for breeding.

William 'Compo' Simmonite, *Last of the Summer Wine*

You're going to have to start taking pleasure in the misfortune of others, Kenneth, or you're going to have a long and unhappy old age.

Blanche Hunt, to Ken Barlow, *Coronation Street*

—She gave me a dirty look and stormed off in a huff...I went down t'canal bank, sat on a bollard and fanned meself with me cap until it went dark.
—There's nought like a good bollard to sit on when you're feeling down in t'dumps. I'd 'ave 'ad one in our front parlour only Edna said it'd cost a fortune in loose covers.

Carter Brandon and Uncle Mort, I Didn't Know You Cared

I suppose I do get sad, but not for too long. I just look in the mirror and go, 'What a fucking good-looking fuck you are.' And then I brighten up.

Liam Gallagher

There is a lot of sorrow in the world. Most of it, luckily, is in 'EastEnders'.

Nancy Banks-Smith

The Greatest Gift That We Possess: **Happiness**

I'm only happy stood in the middle of a cricket field.

Dickie Bird

—Morrissey, I want to thank you. You've made me and so many people happy.
—Well, I didn't mean to.

Awestruck Fan and Morrissey, The Importance of Being Morrissey

One of Mrs Winterson's favourite phrases was: 'Why be happy when you could be normal?'... She distrusted happiness; happiness was a siren song, a false light. The pursuit of happiness was not written into her constitution.

Jeanette Winterson

—Where and when were you happiest?
—21 May 1959.

Interviewer and Morrissey, born 22 May 1959

I had a hit punk record when I was 19 called 'Jilted John'. It has become known as 'Gordon is a Moron'. It should have made me happy, but I didn't relax and take loads of drugs. I bought a five-bedroom house in Manchester with dry rot.

Graham Fellows

The secret of happiness is to plant a seed and watch it grow. You can grow a family, a show, a business, but you do something and see it bloom. The other thing is, you must feel *necessary*.

Ken Dodd

The secret of happiness is to live within your income and pay your bills on time.

Margaret Thatcher

This obsession with being happy is one of the curses of Western civilisation. I need to be discontented. I need stress. I need crises.

Glenda Jackson

I can never feel happy when I am *expected* to feel happy... something in me resists the *calendar expectation* of happiness. *Merry Christmas yourself!* – it mutters as it shapes a ghastly grin.

J.B. Priestley

Constant and repetitive fulfilment is not good for the human spirit. We all need rain and good old depression. Life can't be all beer and skittles.

Morrissey

I mean what's so fulfilling about fulfilment anyway?

Maureen Lipman

Is It Cos I Is Northern? Northern Pride and Prejudice

The commissioning editor said: 'You'll never appear on television.' I said: 'You're about eight million pounds too fucking late.'

Bernard Manning

—How many Pakistanis can you fit in a mini?
—Well, it's obvious – four and possibly a small child.

Bernard Right On, aka John Thomson

Dr Mahmud gave them tablets to me. Dr Mahmud's a Pakistani, you know – but he's very open about it.

Nana, *The Royle Family*

Whatever happened to the 'Black and White Minstrel Show'? It truly was a ground-breaking series. You never saw black people on television before that. It was ahead of its time.

Mrs Merton, aka Caroline Aherne

—You want to marry a miner? But they're all negroes!
—No, no, mother, that's the coal-dust. Underneath, their skin is as white as ours.

Lady Patience and Isobel Hardacre, *Brass*

When Enoch Powell said, 'Go home, black man,' I said, 'I've got a hell of a long wait for a bus to Barnsley.'

Charlie Williams

That kind of patriotism which consists in hating all other nations.

Mrs Gaskell, *Sylvia's Lovers*

You know, the sort of people who start sentences with, 'I'm not being racist, but...'

Paul Heaton

I don't understand why the BNP want to be in the European Parliament, because they're always gonna be sat next to foreigners, aren't they? Unless that might cure them. They go over there and think, 'Oh, it's quite nice here, the people are really friendly...I'm no longer a racist.'

Jason Manford, on the British National Party

There's a black fella, a Pakistani and a Jew in a nightclub 'avin' a drink. What a fine example of an integrated community.

Bernard Right On, aka John Thomson

Pat Wall, chairman of Bradford Trades Council said...he didn't think the
Asians would integrate for years and years, not until they threw off religion
and that wasn't all that likely – not when there wasn't anything else to put
in its place.

Beryl Bainbridge, *English Journey*, 1984

—There's just something about the Japanese I don't trust. Maybe it's
because me Uncle Fred was in Changi prison.
—Is that why you don't like cockneys, cos your Cousin Tom's in
Wormwood Scrubs?
—Every family's got a black sheep. I don't like cockneys because they're
southern.

Terry Collier and Bob Ferris, *Whatever Happened to the Likely Lads?*

Once, we took the family caravan off to Austria, but it was too 'Sound of
Music' for me. My sister had always made me watch Julie Andrews on
Sunday afternoons when 'Dr No' was on the other side, so I decided to
take against the place. But if you're going to be biased against an entire
nation, I think it's good to have a novel reason, rather than just blind
hatred, and that's mine.

Ross Noble

If we're honest, I think we're all a bit racist, aren't we? I know I am. There
are some races that I hate. One of them that I really hate, *fucking* hate –
the egg and spoon race.

Nick Margerrison

I've noticed with this country, basically, everybody hates everybody who's
about 45 minutes away... so, Manchester and Liverpool hate each other,
Portsmouth and Southampton, Glasgow and Edinburgh... Apart from
when there's someone a little bit further away...so, Manchester and

Liverpool, we don't get on, until we see someone from Yorkshire and then we go, 'Well, we're both from the North West.' And then we meet someone from down south and then all three of us are, like, 'Well, we're all Northerners now, aren't we?' And then we meet someone from Scotland, 'Yeah, well, we're English.' Somebody from France, 'We're British.' Someone from America, 'We're European.' The only time the world is gonna be friends is when we get invaded by aliens. We'll all have to be mates, 'We're human.'

Jason Manford

She Knows, You Know: Intelligence

You get depressed sometimes and begin to believe there aren't any real, old fashioned idiots left, and then, out of the blue, comes a genuine, 14-carat, gilt-edged barmpot!

Norman Clegg, *Last of the Summer Wine*

Colin Backhouse said Michael Donovan worked for him between 1989 and 1991 and he'd once sent him to put £20 of diesel in his pick-up only to see him then driving past the firm's premises again and again. When he asked him why, Donovan said he could only fit £18.48 of fuel into the tank so kept driving around until he could squeeze in the other £1.52.

Daily Mirror

He's a thick as a welder's sandwich.

Alan Snell

If you were any thicker, you'd set.

Ken Dixon, *Early Doors*

17

I know folk think I'm simple. What I say to them is that I'd rather be simple and 'ave me pleasures than know everything and be miserable, like Ena Sharples.

Minnie Caldwell, *Coronation Street*

That show, *In Our Time*, that you do on Radio 4... have you any idea what you're really talking about on it? Be honest: is it in code?

Steve Wright (F) to Melvyn Bragg, *Steve Wright Show*, BBC Radio 2

I can only give the honourable and learned gentleman the words I used. I cannot give him the intellectual apparatus to appreciate what they mean.

Harold Wilson, prime minister, to Sir Samuel Knox Cunningham (F)

Mother is far too clever to understand anything she does not like.

Arnold Bennett

When I have to listen to somebody from one of those...'think tanks', I cannot help remembering that verdict of the 'Tao Te Ching': 'Extreme cleverness is as bad as stupidity.'

J.B. Priestley

Professor Stephen Hawking came to my club... His brain is the best in the world. I wanted to talk to him about the universe but he just wanted to watch the girls.

Peter Stringfellow

Bigger Than Jesus: Ego

I wouldn't say I was the best football manager in the business. But I was in the top one.

Brian Clough

There's only one head bigger than his – Birkenhead.

Scouse saying

What I didn't know was that he had a temper and ego you could build a house on.

Cherie Blair, on Alastair Campbell

People say I'm the son of God, but it isn't true – my Nigel is.

Brian Clough

I'm not like John Lennon, who thought he was the great Almighty. I just think I'm John Lennon.

Noel Gallagher

Annie Walker'd attend her own funeral if God let 'er.

Albert Tatlock, *Coronation Street*

If egotism means a terrific interest in one's self, egotism is absolutely essential to efficient living.

Arnold Bennett

Gettin' On: Ambition

If you don't want to be the biggest band in the world, you may as well pack it in now.

Noel Gallagher

I have quite simple ambitions. I can't see the point in bungee jumping or doing something extreme like that when I haven't learned to make stock yet. It'd be awful to die in a bungee-related accident thinking: should have done stock before this – should have gone up in stages.

Alun Cochrane

Where I come from, your biggest ambition would be to grow the biggest carrot.

Nick Park, on growing up in Preston

Two ambitions were yet to be fulfilled, number one being to possess my own overcoat, which would keep me warm through the winter, and number two being, when rationing was a thing of the past, to live a life of thickly buttered toast.

Eric Sykes, *If I Don't Write It, Nobody Else Will*

So I put my foot down. I told him it was time he took his opportunities. I told him the world was his oyster. He said he's allergic to seafood.

Flo Capp, on Andy

4

Success and Failure

I'm totally accepting of rejection. It's almost like the Eskimos, I've got 90 different words for rejection. Rejection doesn't have the same sting for me. Rejection's like sunshine, it's just there.

Johnny Vegas

What I most dislike about myself is the fact that I think I'm capable of achieving anything. If somebody came up to me and said, 'We're just having a bet over there and my mate reckons that you couldn't swim the English Channel.' And I'd say, 'Really? Gimme the fuckin' trunks!' Now I can't swim, but I'd still give it a go.

Noel Gallagher

Why, put him in the middle of a moor, with nothing in the world but his shirt, and you could not prevent him being anything he liked.

T.H. Huxley (F), on William Ewart Gladstone

When Manchester narrowly failed to secure the Olympic games a few years back, the stunned crowds gathered in the city centre to hear the International Olympic Committee's verdict merely blinked, swallowed hard, and burst into a spontaneous rendition of Monty Python's 'Always Look On The Bright Side Of Life'. We know how to take our knocks up North.

Judy Finnigan

I knew I'd conquered America when Mike Tyson told me I was one mean lady.

Anne Robinson

It's pretty devastating to become a chronic alcoholic and lose custody of your child. So many profiles have said, 'Despite that, look what she's done,' whereas they should have said, 'Because of that.'

Anne Robinson

Unlike their grandad – who once shared an outside lavatory with nine other families – my three children have six lavatories to choose between. When your entire family can visit the lavatory at the same time and you've got a bog to spare, you know you've made it.

Chris Donald, co-founder of *Viz* magazine

Communication

Accent and Language

If Father Christmas were to speak, he'd have a northern accent – cosy, big and heartfelt.

Jenny Eclair

Vivienne Westwood's voice is as sweet and gormless as a lollypop lady's... as northern and homely as an episode of 'Coronation Street' sponsored by Tetley tea.

Andrew Billen (F)

Ted Hughes's voice is a mixture of Heathcliffe and God.

Andrew Motion (F)

People, by which I mean television producers, imagine northern speech simply as standard English with a dirty dishcloth accent.

Alan Bennett

I was bathing my four-year-old grandson, product of my Yorkshire son and his Kentish wife. She called out, 'Time to get out of the bath (barth),' and my grandson said pityingly, 'She means bath (rhyming with hath), but she can't help it, she's from down South.'

Sylvia Crookes

You cannot try to adopt a Yorkshire accent because unless you are from Yorkshire you will shorten the word 'the' to a 't', like Robert Carlyle did in 'The Full Monty'. That's wrong... In Yorkshire the word 'the' is replaced by the briefest pause and a small nod of the head.

Jeremy Clarkson

Accent has got a lot to do with the terrain of the land... In Liverpool, you block your nose, cos you don't want all those smells going in; in Hull, you've got the docks, so you close your nose, but it's also very flat. It's also got a slight posh edge to it, so they say things like: 'I'm making a fern curl' (phone call).

Maureen Lipman

A woman goes into a hairdresser's in Newcastle and says, 'Can I have a perm, please?' And the hairdresser goes, 'I wandered lonely as a cloud...'

Ted Robbins

Russell Harty came from Blackburn... He used to say 'Shall you' instead of 'Will you', a lorry became a 'lurry', and even then the phrase 'You are – are you not' was in common usage.

Richard Whiteley, *Himoff!*

Whenever I meet someone with a Somerset burr, I always imagine that in the next five minutes I'm going to be tied to a candlelit table, with a goat, and raped.

Jeremy Clarkson

I cannot bring myself to vote for a woman who has been voice-trained to speak to me as though my dog has just died.

Keith Waterhouse, on Margaret Thatcher

I heard a man say, 'It's awfully nice to see you,' and it occurred to me that it would actually be impossible to say those words in a northern accent even if you wanted to.

Andrew Martin

We don't speak with a plum in the mouth. Those who do went. We don't and we stayed at home.

Fred Trueman, on why he and a fellow player were omitted from the England cricket team to play in a Test match

Words and Grammar

All men are fools, and what makes them so is having beauty like what I have got.

Glenda Jackson, as Cleopatra, *Morecambe and Wise Show*

Not 'what', '*who*'. Didn't they learn you no grammar at school?

Hilda Ogden, *Coronation Street*

Granville, how do you spell p-p-p-p-p-pepper? Is it six ps or seven?

Arkwright, *Open All Hours*

—Which words or phrases do you most overuse?
—'No I won't', 'Why should I?', 'What's the point?' and 'I'd like to terminate our agreement'.

Interviewer and Morrissey

—What is the French for 'apple'?
—Pomme.
—'Two apples'?
—Pomme pomme.

Richard 'Stinker' Murdoch (F) and Arthur Askey

What's French for 'cul-de-sac?' Why have we got it? Get rid of it! It should be in English. It should say: 'You'll-have-to-back-out.'

Mick Miller

Everybody's talking French. I don't understand.

Geoffrey Boycott, during his trial in Grasse, France

It is no exaggeration to describe plain English as a fundamental tool of government.

Margaret Thatcher

My grandad had a huge dictionary and when we went round to visit him I'd have to open it randomly, put my finger on a word and then use that word in context the next time I saw him.

Vic Reeves

You'll have to excuse Gazza. He's got a very small vocabulary.

Lawrie McMenemy, after Paul Gascoigne said, 'Fuck off, Norway,' on TV, 1992

Over The Garden Wall: Gossip

Flippin' street we live in! You only 'ave to 'ave a bath an' everyone knows if you get your toe stuck in the tap!

David Barlow, *Coronation Street*

They've bin talkin' about me ever since I put me first pair o' nylons on.

Elsie Tanner, *Coronation Street*

In the space of a few moments you could hear a whole character dissected, assassinated and chucked in the bin, to be plucked out and redeemed in one small sentence. Thus my mother, in a discussion with Margo concerning Aunt Nellie, would say how lacking in depth Nellie was, too dour, a touch of the martyr. And Auntie Margo, heaping on coals of fire, would mention incidents of cunning and deception, my mother nodding her head all the while in agreement until just as Nellie lay unravelled before my eyes, Auntie Margo would say, 'By heck, but you can't fault her sponge cake.'

Beryl Bainbridge, *English Journey*

There've bin times when Elsie Tanner's life's kept mine going. I've a lot to thank her for.

Ena Sharples, *Coronation Street*

—What's the most outrageous piece of gossip you've heard about yourself?
—Someone once claimed I was not really a Yorkshireman!

Aftab Siddik and William Hague

I have a talent for eavesdropping and it's amazing what you learn while waiting to pay for your fruit juice.

Morrissey

Deaf People: wearing oven gloves outdoors is an ideal way to stop strangers from eavesdropping on your conversation.

Top tip, *Viz* magazine

Run along, the curtains won't twitch themselves!

Blanche Hunt, *Coronation Street*

Insults

You gormless, clueless drip of a mop handle!

Agnes Fairchild, *Brass*

You flea-brained, second-hand elastic bandage!

Agnes Fairchild, *Brass*

You cannot insult me. God got there first.

Johnny Vegas

Like being savaged by a dead sheep.

Denis Healey, on being criticized by Geoffrey Howe (F) in the House

After I joined Celtic football club I was walking down the street in Glasgow when someone shouted, 'Fenian bastard!' I had to look it up – Fenian, that is.

Mick McCarthy, Yorkshire-born Republic of Ireland manager, 1996

—I didn't come here to be insulted.
—Where do you normally go?

Robin Day and Eric Morecambe, The Morecambe and Wise Show

—Go to Hell!
—Any message?

Freda and John Rook

Graham Greene put carrots in a Lancashire hotpot.

Anthony Burgess

Swearing

Sweet Baby Jesus, Mother Teresa, Billy Liar and Miami Vice!

Brian Potter, Phoenix Nights

Hecky plonk!

Thora Hird

—He's filthy and he's fucking foul-mouthed.
—Eh, there's no need for that language, please. I've got a photograph of the wife in my wallet.

Committee Member and Brian Potter, Phoenix Nights

I was criticized for swearing on television. The word I used was 'bloody', which, where I come from in Yorkshire, is practically the only surviving adjective.

Maureen Lipman

'Fuck!' she said when she found out Blair had made her Foreign Secretary...
Margaret Beckett swears a lot, according to former colleagues. 'Vividly
and with great dignity,' says one. 'She avoids the "c" word generally but
would never say as weak a word as "bloody".'

The Independent

A vocabulary that would take the feathers off a hoody crow.

Lillian Beckwith

I would like to know who Nora is and why the poor woman so often
bursts into flames.

Jeffrey Miller (F)

Telephone

Oh, no, just look at this phone bill. It's all that Ruby's fault. She does
nothing but listen, listen, listen!

Flo Capp

—Did Thelma call?
—No.
—Are you sure?
—Positive. We haven't got a phone.

Bob Ferris and Terry Collier, *The Likely Lads*

—I'm not a phone person. I can't quite get used to the telephone.
—Why? Lack of intimacy?
—Lack of interest. There's usually a person on the other end.

Morrissey and Interviewer

D'you ever have that thing where you think your phone's ringing in your pocket, like a vibration, and you check and there's no phone call there – it's a phantom phone call? That's actually a psychological condition: it's called 'loneliness'.

Jeff Green

I rang Directory Enquiries for The Wig and Pen Club. The operator apologetically informed me that there was no listing for a Pen Club in Wigan.

Raj Kothari (F)

The ban on mobile phones in British hospitals must remain. Otherwise the corridors will echo with cries of, 'I'm on the trolley.'

John Burscough

Texting is the devil. It takes over your life. I sit, at night, with me phone on th'arm of t'couch, looking every few seconds just to see if someone's texted me. 'What R U watching?' 'Corrie.' 'I know. We're in the same room.'

Peter Kay

Why have we got predictive texting? Why do we need it? We don't have predictive talking – but it would be great if we did: 'Where did you go today?' 'Today, me? I ~~wallabied, wanked,~~ walked to the ~~sharons, shits,~~ shops... I reckon that's what Tourette's is – it's just predictive talking people can't turn off.

Lee Mack

The more we elaborate our means of communication, the less we communicate.

J.B. Priestley

Writer

—You could be another Brontë sister.
—I can't sing.

Morecambe and Wise

True, if you find yourself born in Barnsley, and then set your sights on being Virginia Woolf it is not going to be roses all the way.

Alan Bennett, Writing Home

Maybe I should concentrate on being the second Philip Larkin. 'They fuck you up, your mum and dad.' But mine didn't. That's the trouble, perhaps. They gave me a very happy loving contented childhood – the bastards.

Aspiring Author, Uncle Mort's North Country

We don't want literature, my friend: we want a bestseller.

Anthony Burgess

In 1978 he announced that he was embarking on a book about his home town, Sunderland, but somehow ended up producing a photo-essay about women's breasts, a subject on which he seemed to be something of an expert.

Times obituary on Alan Brien, journalist

My father could neither read nor write, and when I handed him my first novel to look at he turned it round and round in his hands and said, with some stupefaction: 'Bloody hell, Alan, you've written a book! You'll never have to work again!'

Alan Sillitoe (the novel was Saturday Night and Sunday Morning)

I said to my publishers: 'What are you going to do if all my books sell out?' and they said: 'Oh, we'll print another ten.'

Eric Sykes

Beryl is getting down to her new novel. She can't accept social engagements as they inevitably lead to getting tired and emotional.

Message on Beryl Bainbridge's answering machine

Poetic Off Licence

Hovis Presley, title of poetry collection

The other day I met Hovis Presley, a fine poet and a true gentleman. So I had a drink with all three of them.

John Cooper Clarke

—I can't stand poetry. I was put off it at an early age. The only poem I ever wrote, I got a good hiding for.
—You shouldn't have written it on the lavatory wall.

Terry Collier and Bob Ferris, *Whatever Happened to the Likely Lads?*

—Melvyn Bragg, how many novels have you written?
—If memory serves, about a dozen.
—[*to the audience*] If you've ever read a novel by Melvyn Bragg, raise your hand.
[*about three hands go up*] Slow down, Melv! Give the rest of us a chance to catch up!

Dame Edna Everage (F) and Melvyn Bragg, *An Audience With Dame Edna Everage*

The Book What I Wrote: Books and Reading

Whenever I want a good read, I get one of Jeffrey Archer's novels and stand on it so I can reach the good books.

Steven Norris

I have a loathing for any book that doesn't have a swastika, a gun and a girl in a bikini on the cover.

Jeremy Clarkson

This book is environmentally positive... It can be used as a pillow, a breeding cage for dormice, a filing system for your pancakes... and pressing very small pairs of trousers.

Mike Harding, *The Armchair Anarchist's Almanac*

The Brontë sisters were the Jilly Coopers of yesteryear, with their tales of romance and unrequited love.

Mrs Merton, aka Caroline Aherne

I've always felt reading romantic novels was a bit like eating a whole box of chocolates, or going to bed with a rotter. You can't stop during the act because it's so nice, but afterwards you wish you hadn't.

Jilly Cooper

Agatha Christie has given more pleasure in bed than any other woman.

Nancy Banks-Smith

When you come to the end of a crime novel, something at least in this huge, chaotic world has been settled.

J.B. Priestley

—What is your favourite book?
—My pension book.

Interviewer and Sir Jimmy Savile

The most invigorating form of reading matter is, of course, a will.

Nancy Banks-Smith

I hope this book turns out to be 'Mein Kampf' for the Hollyoaks generation.

Mark E. Smith, on his book, *Renegade*

—What books are currently by your bedside?
—'Anxiety and Panic Attacks – Their Cause and Cure'; 'Understanding Obsessions and Compulsions'; 'Coping With Anxiety and Depression'; 'How to Heal Depression': 'Daily Reflections' by Members of Alcoholics Anonymous; 'How to Stop Worrying'.

Reporter and Paul Gascoigne

Have you read, 'The Rubyiat of Omar Sharif'?

Eli Pledge, *Nearest and Dearest*

—You're always reading books! Why can't you read important things?
—Such as?
—The small print on the bottom of our mortgage form.
—Oh, that. I don't reckon much to the plot.

Pat and Carter Brandon, *I Didn't Know You Cared*

News and Media

The Daily Lamp Post

Gromit's newspaper of choice, *A Close Shave*

I'm worried about Granville. He keeps sneaking off to the bog with the 'Manchester Guardian'. Why, when I've struggled to bring him up orthodox 'Yorkshire Post'. It's no place for a formative mind, that – they talk about cannabis as if it was ice-cream.

Arkwright, *Open All Hours*

I fancied journalism from the moment I saw Rosalind Russell perch on the news editor's desk and cross her legs with a silky slither like snakes mating. Her hat, against all laws of gravity, was on the side of her head. You did not associate her with gravity at all. That, I thought, will do for me.

Nancy Banks-Smith

Journalists say a thing that they know isn't true, in the hope that if they keep on saying it long enough it will be true.

Arnold Bennett

There used to be a rule of thumb in the old BBC radio newsroom that, in terms of foreign newsworthiness, 60,000 dead in floods in China equalled 90 dead in a hotel fire in Italy, equalled 2 Brits slightly injured in a car crash in Brittany.

Jeremy Paxman

The archetypal tabloid story is a piece of high-precision engineering, with the predictability accurate to within 1/1000th of an inch, the hackneyed phraseology polished like old brass, and puns worn smooth with age gliding effortlessly into place like the moving parts of a well-oiled Victorian donkey engine.

Keith Waterhouse

Any man who can afford to buy a newspaper should not be allowed to own one.

Roy Hattersley

Places

North/South Divide

Is there anyone here from the north? I ask you, what's the point of having a north/south divide if you're not going to police it?

Jimmy Carr (F)

I'd like to apologize to viewers in the North. It must be awful for them.

Continuity Announcer (F), *Victoria Wood, As Seen on TV*

Southerners always regard having lived in the north as a strange medical phenomenon or the reason for having an unusual diet or peculiar haircut.

Morrissey, *Melody Maker*

When one of us passes on, I shall move south to live with my daughter.

Irene Wilkes

Terry, you belong here [in the North East]. You always said this is the only place you feel comfortable in. If you get on a train to King's Cross, you feel jittery by Doncaster.

Bob Ferris, *Whatever Happened to the Likely Lads?*

A Geordie friend of mine advised that when judging Southerners we must always remember 'that they have not had the benefit of our disadvantages.'

Harry Pearson

Have you ever heard anyone boast about coming from Essex or Hampshire? Some Southerners are so ashamed of their true origins that they claim allegiance to Middlesex – a county that no longer even exists.

Roy Hattersley

The episode that for me typifies North versus South in English history took place outside Hull in 1642. The representative of a Southern government demanded entry into the city to levy taxes to pay for the extravagant lifestyle of Charles I. The burghers of the port slammed the City Gate in his face.

Roy Hattersley

Why move from the North to the South? You go to London and within ten minutes you've got black snot. If you live in the North of England, next time you go to London, spend ten minutes there, then blow your nose. It's black.

Justin Moorhouse

Northerners don't live in the North, because the North already lives in them. Penny Lane is in their ears and in their eyes.

Nancy Banks-Smith

To my mother, anyone who lived south of Derby was a cockney.

Alan Titchmarsh, *Nobbut a Lad*

I had not reckoned on foreign service when I joined up.

Beau Brummell (F), resigning his commission on learning that his regiment
was to be sent from Brighton to Manchester, 1798

—What do you miss about Manchester?
—I miss the kind of things that nobody could understand why they could
be missed. I miss the grey slate of the sky. But you're Southern – you
wouldn't understand.

Jools Holland (F) and Morrissey, *Later With Jools Holland*

When you're Northern, you're Northern for ever and you're instilled with
a certain feel for life that you can't get rid of.

Morrissey

I'm really chained to those iron bridges. I'm really chained to the pier. I'm
persistently on some disused clearing in Wigan. I shall be buried there, I'm
sure, and I shall be glad to go at that point.

Morrissey

London

I rang me mum the other week. She said, 'Where are you?' I said, 'I'm in
London.' She said, 'You don't sound like you're in London.' I said, 'What
d'you want, Chas 'n' Dave singing 'Rabbit' behind me?'

Peter Kay

—Where were you born?
—London.
—What part?
—All of me.

Sandy Powell and Young Boy (F)

I always get a bit homesick when I go down to London so what I do is, I get on the tube and sit on the Northern Line for a bit.

Jason Manford

London is just a disparate mass of disparate people linked by a tube network.

Stuart Maconie

First time I went to London, I got stuck on the underground. I got on the escalator, there was a sign: 'Dogs must be carried.' Could I find a dog? Could I fuck.

Dave Spikey

If you want to freak the hell out of anyone in London, just get on the tube and say, 'Good morning!' Aaghh...

Stephen Tompkinson

Halifax suits me fine. London's all rush, rush, rush and tip, tip, tip.

Percy Shaw, inventor of catseyes

Places – General

Prince Charles went to the North of England to make a speech, wearing Davy Crockett headgear. At the end of his address, someone went up to him and said: 'Brilliant, but what an extraordinary thing you've got on your head.' Prince Charles said: 'It was Mama's idea. I told her I was going to Scunthorpe, and she said, "Wear the fox hat."'

Clement Freud (F)

—Nancy Riley's moved to Shrewsbury.
—Where's Shrewsbury?
—League Division Three, about six from the top.

Terry Collier and Bob Ferris, Whatever Happened to the Likely Lads?

If I were to choose a place to live, I would certainly prefer Wolverhampton to Florence.

Roy Hattersley

Cheshire is just like England, only there's no class system, just the haves and the haves-even-more. Cleaners, I suspect, are bussed in from Moss Side and then shot.

Jeremy Clarkson

Time passed slowly like a month in the doldrums or a day in Gravesend.

Nancy Banks-Smith

They say that men become attached even to Widnes.

A.J.P. Taylor

What I would say to people in the North: 'Not every town has to have a cake named after it.' That infuriates them cos there's two or three, which is enough to make them think there might be loads.

Stewart Lee (F)

Lancashire

So you're down from Lancashire, where the real people live?

J.L. Carr

—Where were you born?
—Blackpool.
—Have you lived in Blackpool all your life?
—Not yet.

Nicky (F) and Jack Parker, *Funny Bones*

Blackpool's main use to society will one day be as an alternative to custody once the prisons are full.

Simon Heffer (F)

I love Bolton... I can go to the chippy in my slippers. You can't do that down London, you'd get arrested.

Peter Kay

Welcome to Oldham, Home of the Tubular Bandage

City slogan

—How could God make Accrington?
—Well, it doesn't matter because in the Second Coming, it will be
destroyed.

Jeanette Winterson and her Mother

I once got a puncture in a place called Hindley Green, on the outskirts of
Wigan. I pulled into a garage and said, 'Have you got an Airline?' He said,
'Fuck off, we've not even got a bus station.'

Dave Spikey

Here's a local joke: a sophisticated man of the world, possibly from
Chorley or Bolton, is attempting to entice his Wiganer workmate to the
pub at lunchtime. 'They've got a lunchtime special on; a pie, a pint and a
woman, 80 pence. Eighty pence!' 'Ah,' replies the Wiganer, eyes narrowed
in suspicion. 'Whose pies are they, though?'

Stuart Maconie, *Cider With Roadies*

The only reason meat pies have got a little hole in the top of them is so
Wigan people can pick four up at once.

Dave Spikey

Wigan has just been designated E.U. Capital of Pies... Every other shop's a
pie shop: Pies R Us, W.H.Pies, PIEKEA... They've even got a Piestretcher –
I mean, I'm not an expert, but to me that's a pasty.

Dave Spikey

That string of mill towns that seems to run one end to the other of
Lancashire, I don't know what you do with those... Are they worth
regenerating? I think the most one could hope for is another plague,

another bout of Russian flu that depletes the population by twenty million and then we could demolish all those places.

Brian Sewell (F)

The qualities of Salford men and women shine through the adversity of their everyday lives. They were, and still are, people with courage, determination, wit and compassion, and they have an unrivalled ability to see through falseness and to expose insincerity.

Hazel Blears, maiden speech in the House of Commons on becoming MP for Salford in 1997

Mancs: **Manchester**

It's great to be in Manchester – home of Oasis, Smiths, and other high street retail outlets.

Tony Ferrino (F), aka Steve Coogan

Manchester was pretty grey in the 70s. I liked them days. It's turning touristy now.

Mark E. Smith

You can spot the BBC employees who move up to Manchester. They walk in the corner shop, these children's TV presenters in stripey jumpers: 'Oh, you're Mark E. Smith, my brother had one of your records, I've just moved up here and it's wonderful!' They soon learn.

Mark E. Smith

Manchester, that's not such a nice place.

Queen Elizabeth II (F), to a Russian student who told her she had been there

I spent Christmas in Manchester, just to go into the Royal Mail depot to see all the postmen going, 'Sorted! Sorted!'

Milton Jones (F)

The one good thing you can say for Manchester is that it's not Liverpool.

Richard Littlejohn (F)

This rivalry between Liverpool and Manchester is unnecessary. Between Liverpool and Manchester, what is there? Warrington. And let's be honest, before the Swedes built a shop, we didn't even know it was there.

John Bishop

Scousers: Liverpool

Ladies and gentlemen, we are at 35,000ft. Please hold on to your wallets, we're flying over Liverpool.

EasyJet pilot (F), announcement to passengers

Somewhere between 'murder' and 'suicide' there is a place called Merseyside.

Milton Jones (F)

You've got to be a comedian to live there... I call it Mirthy-side.

Ken Dodd

Anything you say may be used in Everton against you.

John Lennon

Liverpool is a kind of collision caused by the English trying to get out while the Irish are trying to get in.

Nancy Banks-Smith

Famous Liverpudlians ('Scousers') include Jimmy Tarbuck ('Tarby'), Cilla Black ('Cilla') and Les Dennis ('that bloke off the telly'). Cilla and Tarby, true to their proud roots in Everton and Toxteth, still live very close by in Marbella.

Humphrey Lyttelton (F), *I'm Sorry I Haven't a Clue*

Oh, those poor shopkeepers!

Margaret Thatcher, on seeing the first pictures of rioting and looting in Toxteth, 1981

I am so tied to Liverpool by the past, by memories of family and beginnings, that I still think of it as home. If an uprising broke out in Liverpool, and God knows it may do, like those exiled Jews who returned to defend their country during the Six-Day War, I would rush to the barricades.

Beryl Bainbridge, *English Journey*

Tykes: Yorkshire

I'm from Yorkshire. I'm the full Brontë.

Barry Cryer

How can I best define a Yorkshireman: A lady of the night says she'll do anything on earth if you can describe it in ten words. A Liverpudlian comes in and says, 'Nuzzle my crevices!' So she does and £10 is exchanged. Then a Cockney comes in and says, 'Lick me everywhere!' So she does and £10 is exchanged. Then the Yorkshireman comes in and says: 'Paint my 'ouse!'

Maureen Lipman

45

A Yorkshireman is someone born within the sound of Bill Bowes.

Mike Carey

I don't speak French. I don't speak English. I am from Yorkshire.

Geoffrey Boycott

I can speak a bit o' Yorkshire: 'How much?!'

Ken Dodd

—Which Yorkshire sportsman/woman would you take for lunch?
—Robert Mugabe! If you spell Mugabe backwards you get E-ba-gum, so he must be a Yorkshireman, mustn't he?

Reporter and Sir Jimmy Savile, *Yorkshire Post*

If you're a Yorkshireman, you either marry a girl from Yorkshire or from New York. The Yorkshire girl is used to it and the New Yorker doesn't know any better.

Betsy Bell (F), New Yorker married to a Yorkshireman

You can never impress a Yorkshireman.

Lady Ingilby, *Yorkshire Post*

The flowers of Yorkshire are like the women of Yorkshire. Every stage of their growth has its own beauty, but the last phase is always the most glorious. Then very quickly they all go to seed.

Chris Harper, quoting John Clarke, *Calendar Girls*

All Yorkshire people call a spade a shovel and, when roused, dig the graves of people who irritate them.

Jean Rook

I hold Yorkshire to be a mistake.

James Agate

Several world-famous comic writers were born in Leeds. Everybody in the city has heard of Alan Bennett and Barry Cryer has heard of him as well.

Humphrey Lyttelton (F), *I'm Sorry I Haven't a Clue*

Tell someone that you live, or have lived, in Leeds, and they are quite likely to say, 'Well, it's easy to get out of.'

Alan Bennett

I became a great runner because if you're a kid in Leeds and your name is Sebastian you've got to become a great runner.

Sebastian Coe

Founded on textiles, until 1969 Leeds had the world's largest surviving woollen mill. Then someone pulled a loose thread and the whole building unravelled.

Humphrey Lyttelton (F), *I'm Sorry I Haven't a Clue*

In Todmorden, we used to have the highest UFO sightings rate in Britain. I believe it was just wishful thinking though. No, they weren't just wishing that they'd seen a UFO either, they were wishing one would remove them to an entirely different universe.

Steve Hanson

Hull is the kind of place that you are from and not the kind of place you choose to live.

Simon Mills

You know what they say about Hull: 'When a man is tired of Hull, he's... normal.'

Maureen Lipman

Hull highs: liquorice tablets, Beverley Road baths, direct route to Amsterdam. Low points: being beaten up by teenage girls on the way to the newsagents.

C. Chapman

—You're from York, which is the most beautiful place. It has the Mumbles, or is it the Grumbles, or the Fumbles?
—It's the Shambles.

Sherrie Hewson and Mark Addy, *Loose Women*

Some people say that York is soft; the 'Guildford of the North' I once heard it called, but they've probably never been standing on Micklegate at chucking out time on Saturday night.

Andrew Martin

—Yorkshire is not even one of the superpowers competing for the ideological leadership of the world.
—It all went wrong when they sacked Boycott.

Walter 'Foggy' Dewhurst and Norman Clegg, *Last of the Summer Wine*

Geordies and Mackems: Tyneside

Don Warrington says he has to go to Newcastle for Christmas. I say I like Newcastle. 'Why? It's all vomit and love-bites.'

Alan Bennett, *Writing Home*

In America they once asked me what my home town of Newcastle was like and I said it was a nice place to bring up your food. I thought it was hilarious at the time – but the people living there did not.

Sting

There's the honour of the Geordie nation to defend at all times, standing arm-in-arm with Jimmy Nail, Alan Shearer, Dame Flora Robson, Ant, Dec and the man who does the voice-overs for Big Brother.

Phil Johnson

It's tough being a Geordie... All that beer to drink, the proper note of genial chirpiness to maintain, and having to remember to say 'like' at the end of every sentence, like.

Phil Johnson

I am a Geordie, which means I come from Newcastle, and we pride ourselves on being very outspoken, very loud, very happy-go-lucky and rough and ready; a bit like Australians really. We have never felt ourselves to be English and we call them Poms as well.

Alun Armstrong

Stockton-on-Tees: Home of the Friction Match

Sign on roundabout in Stockton

49

A Geordie said to me: 'Are yous looking at us?' How many mistakes can you make in one sentence?

Michael McIntyre (F)

The phrase which makes one an instant Geordie is, 'Wey, yer Bugger.' It's a phrase which covers a multiple of meanings, and is as harmless as 'God bless you' in Geordieland.

Joe Ging

I used to live on Amberley Street in Sunderland – as featured on 'Crime Watch' and a 'Panorama Special' on car crime.

Unidentified Mackem

I'm not sure where he is now, but it's either West Hartlepool or the Gold Coast.

F.D. Mason, overheard on a bus

Relationships and Family Life

Men and Women

Northern women are another species. They have come down by a separate genetic route and like the Galapagos turtles (whom some of them resemble) they have developed their own characteristics and attitudes.

Alan Bennett

Women never have young minds. They are born three thousand years old.

Boy, *A Taste of Honey*

Alastair Campbell once said that I had the brains of a man and the emotions of a woman and he found that very difficult. The truth is he didn't like to think that women had equal capacity.

Cherie Blair

I usually make up my mind about a man in ten seconds and I very rarely change it.

Margaret Thatcher

—Is there any difference between men and women?
—I've never seen a man that looked good in a pinafore dress. Unless it was very, very plain with no bust-darts.

Michael Grade (F) and Victoria Wood

In her world, men loved women as the fox loved the hare. And women loved men as the tapeworm loves the gut.

Pat Barker, *Regeneration*

Man is the dog, and woman is the bone. He eats the best of you, and buries the rest of you, and when his dish is empty, he'll dig you up again.

Mrs Hennessey, *The Liver Birds*

Women ruin everything. The only thing that I have done within my house in the last 20 years is to recognize Angola as an independent state.

Brian Clough

A man...is *so* in the way in the house!

Mrs Gaskell, Cranford

They say men can't multi-task but you watch us when we nearly get caught watching porn, we're like ninjas: telly-over, trousers-up, tissues-down-the-couch!

Jason Manford

I'm sick and tired of people coming up to me saying, 'You're a sexist!' I'm not a sexist. I'm a radical feminist. I think you've got to be these days if you want to get your end away.

Paul Calf, aka Steve Coogan

According to feminists, 'All men are potential rapists.' Well, I'm not. I'm a convicted one.

G.B., H.M. Prison, Hull, Viz magazine

—What does a woman want?
—More.

Chris Evans

You should treat women the same way as a Yorkshire batsman used to treat a cricket ball. Don't stroke 'em, don't tickle 'em, just give 'em a ruddy good belt.

Fred Trueman

The cocks may crow, but it's the hen that lays the egg.

Margaret Thatcher

If they ever invent a vibrator that can open pickle jars, men have had it.

Jeff Green

Nowt So Queer: Sexuality

I'm sick o' fellas. Think I'll become a lesbian. At least you get to wear flat shoes.

Lily Savage, aka Paul O'Grady

MUM, I'M GAY

Liverpool banner seen at the Champions League football final

To enquire if I was homosexual was like asking someone who had just crawled across the Sahara Desert whether they preferred Malvern or Perrier water.

Alan Bennett

I'm not gay. Unless you're from Newcastle and by 'gay' you mean, 'owns a coat'.

Jimmy Carr (F)

If he was any further back in the closet, he'd be in Narnia.

Daniel Bryan

You 'Ad Me At "Ey Up': Attraction

Fred used to say, 'Everything I like in life is heavy, dirty or dangerous.' I think he thought I were all three.

Sheila Dibnah, wife of Fred

Pat Phoenix was like a hurricane... You simply wanted to rush towards her bosom, you know, remain there forever.

Morrissey

Gladys Emmanuel is everything I've ever wanted in a woman: a huge chest and a backside like a school-bus. I've got no time for these modern women with no room in the boot.

Arkwright, *Open All Hours*

I was by myself in a Dublin hotel where I was going to meet Harvey Smith for research on my new book. I was wearing dungarees and when he met me on the stairs he said, 'Ee lass, you've got a bum bigger than Ted Edgar's.'

Jilly Cooper

[*suggestively*] —Why don't you come and sit beside me and we'll while away a few of those 15 years...
—Can I just warn you, Roger, I've got really complicated pants on.

Roger Moore and Victoria Wood, *Victoria Wood With All the Trimmings*

If Helen's face could launch a thousand ships, ten thousand might be sunk by Thelma's hips.

Leonard Barras, *Up the Tyne in a Flummox*

I think girls should be the shape and size to fit the spiritual needs of the individual; in my case, rounded, muscular and generating enough body-warmth to cut down the fuel costs in the bedroom.

Arkwright, *Open All Hours*

—I like them 'Gladiator' women on telly.
—I'm with you there, mate. Not only do they look as if they could give you a fantastic seeing to but, unlike most women, they'd 'ave no trouble hanging out the loft window and adjusting your aerial.

Keith and Stan, *Dinnerladies*

I fell in love the first time I saw my wife, Mary, on a bus. I remember thinking, I could look at that face for a long, long time – and I have.

Michael Parkinson, 50 years married

I knew as soon as I saw you climbing the stairs on the all-night bus, I said to meself, she's just my type.

Eli Pledge, *Nearest and Dearest*

[*suggestively*] —Would you like to see where I had my operation?
—If you think I'm going to Liverpool General Hospital this time of night, you're mistaken.

Loose Lady and Roy 'Chubby' Brown

—I've fancied Nora Batty for years. Can't explain it. Must be something chemical.
—Oh. Like Harpic.

William 'Compo' Simmonite and Norman Clegg, *Last of the Summer Wine*

I'm madly in love with Alan Titchmarsh – he's from Ilkley too... We both love gardening and write novels. We've also both been nominated for the bad sex award.

Jilly Cooper

I can't stand smoothies.

Margaret Thatcher

—Tell us, Wally, what's the secret? What does Nora like in a man?
—Total submission!

William 'Compo' Simmonite and Wally Batty, *Last of the Summer Wine*

One night, I bought that film with Sharon Stone, the one where she crosses her legs... The wife said, 'Look at you, you dirty, mucky bastard. Take away her blonde hair, blue eyes, white teeth, 36-D cup and long legs, and what've you got?' I said, 'You!'

Roy 'Chubby' Brown

I can't stand the sight of naked women... I like to see a woman as nature intended her – fur boots, blue duffle coat and one of those hats from Francine Fashions.

Les Brandon, *I Didn't Know You Cared*

Do you like me more than you don't like me or do you not like me more than you do?

Geoffrey Ingham, *A Taste of Honey*

I'll do anything to get the chance to get clasped in the general direction of that regal bosom. Oh, there's a pillow for a man! I could rest me cheeks on that and be comforted right down to the roots of me bare bones. Keep yer modern standards. Try and rest for comfort on a pair of them and you'll finish up with perforated eardrums.

Arkwright, *Open All Hours*

—Why do you do things like that when you know she's only going to hit you with a brush?
—That shows she cares... When she sees me coming she gets palpitations.
—Don't we all.

Walter 'Foggy' Dewhurst and William 'Compo' Simmonite,
Last of the Summer Wine

She certainly knows her rugby league, and her dominoes. And she can sup pints like a good 'un. By gum, she's arf way to being my idea of t'perfect woman: a bloke with big knockers.

Uncle Mort, *I Didn't Know You Cared*

Courting

—Who was that lady I seen you with last night?
—You mean, 'I saw.'
—Sorry. Who was that eyesore I seen you with last night?

Morecambe and Wise

Connie? There's a woman you'd grow a marrow for.

Jack Duckworth, *Coronation Street*

I met her in the tunnel of love. She was digging it. I can see her now, hooking clay from behind her denture-plate.

Les Dawson

—When I went to pick her up last night, she opened the door in her negligee.
—That's a funny place to have a door.

Ernie Wise and Eric Morecambe

Your left leg's Christmas, your right leg's Easter – can I visit you between holidays?

Lee, *Not Going Out*

C'mon love, you're nowt special.

Paul Calf, aka Steve Coogan, useful chat-up line

I was a great womaniser. I tended to hunt alone, like a U-boat going about quietly to operate.

Albert Finney

—Can you catch, love?
—Why?
—Cos I've got a couple of balls coming your way.

Paddy O'Shea and Nightclub Dancer, *Max and Paddy's Road to Nowhere*

'What's the difference between a 12 course Chinese banquet and an egg butty?' he said. 'I don't know,' she replied. 'Do you want to come round for your tea?' he asked.

Hovis Presley, *Sun-dried Tomatoes and Mushy Peas*

—Did you see her home?
—I put me slippers on and walked her to the bus-stop.
—As far as women are concerned, you're hardly Omar Sharif are you?
—If Omar Sharif lived in Gateshead, I doubt he'd be Omar Sharif.

Bob Ferris andTerry Collier, *The Likely Lads*

—I've invited Kate round for dinner. I though you might like to join us.
—Haven't you heard the expression, 'Three's a crowd?'
—'Course I have – I support Wigan.

Lee and Lucy (F), *Not Going Out*

I can't stop thinking about you. We had some good times and bad times. Do you remember when I was sick in the back of that taxi and he threw us out in the middle of the Peak District at two in the morning and all we had was half a can of lager? And there were bad times as well. Like when we didn't have any lager at all.

Paul Calf, aka Steve Coogan

[*Arkwright is up a ladder outside Nurse Gladys's bedroom window*]
—What are you doin' up 'ere?
—Just passin'.

Nurse Gladys Emmanuel and Arkwright, *Open All Hours*

—Have you ever met the girl of your dreams?
—No, I've rather met the girls of my nightmares.

Interviewer and Morrissey

This French girl said, 'We can never be lovers, cos we're friends.' Then the next day, she got drunk and tried to take me mate to bed. And I was like, 'Why did you do that?' And she was like, 'Because I would never have him as a friend.' Oh, wait till I tell him, he'll be gutted.

Johnny Vegas

I have a rule: I won't date anyone young enough to be my son.

Cilla Black

—You were writing to a bloke for ages. What happened there?
—I sent him a picture, like he asked, and then I never heard anything.
—Well, there wasn't much future in it really. Wasn't he in for life?

Denise Best and Cheryl Carroll, *The Royle Family*

Romance

What's that perfume you're wearing, Nurse Gladys Emmanuel? Evening in Plaster-of-Paris, isn't it?

Arkwright, *Open All Hours*

Her mother had just finished the washing and we sat holding hands and watching the moon go down over her father's underpants.

Les Dawson

—Is that all you're doing on your wedding anniversary then, Eddie, going to the pub, and then going for a bag o' chips? It's hardly romantic, is it?
—Show her how much you love her, Eddie. Throw in a fish.

Tanya and Ken Dixon, *Early Doors*

Men, married men, young married men, remember that your wives still enjoy chocolates, sweets, perfume, flowers. Let her see that you haven't forgotten. Mention them occasionally.

Eric Morecambe

Me and Leo had both been brought up in the West Riding together... To this day I have a Valentine card he sent me when I was fourteen. It is covered with roses and bloody hearts. Inside he had written just the words: 'Isn't this awful.'

Jilly Cooper

I wanted love poems, but you couldn't write them; my earlobes nibbled, but you couldn't bite them; you'd only fart and then attempt to light them – things would never have worked.

Victoria Wood

For her birthday, she'd asked him for something romantic yet practical, and sure enough, he'd produced a negligee with a pocket for garden shears.

Hovis Presley, *Sun-dried Tomatoes and Mushy Peas*

How many men will give you a cast iron manhole as a birthday present, and promise you a weighbridge next year?

Sheila Dibnah, wife of Fred

Romance is different all over the world. In France, when a lady is having a romantic interlude, she looks up and says, 'Sacré flippin' bleu!' In Italy, when a lady is having a romantic interlude, she looks up and says, 'Sempre amore!' In Britain, when a lady is having a romantic interlude, she looks up and says, 'That ceiling needs doing!'

Ken Dodd

My girlfriend's always complaining. She says I don't treat her properly. So I took her out for tea and biscuits. She enjoyed it. It was the giving blood she didn't like.

Anthony J. Brown

His previous romantic gestures include pawning his Rolex to buy his girlfriend a boob job.

The Sun, on Mario Marconi, *Big Brother 9*

—She wants to be taken out more.
—Aye, I had a sheepdog like that. I can only think of one advantage women have over sheepdogs: they don't chase cars.

Les Brandon and Uncle Mort, I Didn't Know You Cared

I'd never get out the house if it wasn't for aerobics and emptying t'bin.

Debbie, Early Doors

I tell you what, Cheryl, why don't I take you out on Sunday? I'll show you a proper date: we'll do a car-boot in the morning and then I'll treat you to a full fry-up at the trucker's caf.

Twiggy, The Royle Family

[*in a restaurant*] —Would you like to buy a flower for the lady?
—Fuck off.

Flower Seller and Brian Potter, Phoenix Nights

—Give us a kiss! Come on you daft apeth! [*She kisses him*]
—What's that lipstick taste of?
—Woman, Stanley, *woman*!

Hilda and Stan Ogden, Coronation Street

—Tell me, Nurse Gladys, what would you, in the medical profession, recommend for a lovebite?
—Your own teeth!

Arkwright and Nurse Gladys Emmanuel, Open All Hours

Love

D'you reckon I'm in love with Nora Batty – or is it just sex?

Norman Clegg, *Last of the Summer Wine*

Balzac describes Lancashire as 'the county where women die of love'. I think this is very unlikely.

A.J.P. Taylor

I really liked Solomon, and I was prepared to change religion and give up bacon for him, but when it came to pork pies, I just couldn't make that commitment, so I suppose the love wasn't strong enough.

Cheryl Carroll, *The Royle Family*

Elsie Tanner's heart is where a fella's wallet is – and the bigger the wallet, the more heart she's got.

Hilda Ogden, *Coronation Street*

—What or who is the greatest love of your life?
—Next door's cat.

Interviewer and Morrissey

You need somebody to love you while you're looking for someone to love.

Geoffrey Ingham, *A Taste of Honey*

I always start the day by asking my husband if he loves me.

Anne Robinson, in 2003 (divorced in 2007 after 27 years of marriage)

—We've got five kids, you must have loved me five times at least.
—Only one was love. Two were duty, one was a Christmas party, and one was a trip to Brighton.

Mr and Mrs Boswell, *Bread*

Our love is more precious than the Mona Lisa; you're as close to me as the 'a' to the 'e' in Julius Cæsar.

Bob Wooler

She said, 'Your love just turns me dizzy. Come along big boy, get busy.' But I kept my ukulele in my hand, yes sir, I kept my ukulele in my hand."

George Formby, *With My Ukulele In My Hand*

—What would you do without me?
—I'd probably buy a hamster.

Ernie Wise and Eric Morecambe

Walter! Walter! Lead Me To The Altar! Engagement and Wedding

Time is passing us by, Nurse Gladys Emmanuel. It's no longer springtime. Why don't we get engaged – before we've both got a moustache.

Arkwright, *Open All Hours*

It is easier to choose a cricket bat than pick a wife... A bat has a watermark of quality – the grain... The one basic flaw in the otherwise perfect construction of women is that you can't detect the knots in the grain until it's too late.

Michael Parkinson, *Bats in the Pavilion*

This fella says, 'I've got these two girls, and I don't know which one to marry.' His friend said, 'What religion are you?' He said, 'Protestant.' He said, 'I'm a Catholic, I can help you. Go into our church, kneel down, the Lord will guide you.' The fella goes into the church, he was only in five seconds, he ran out, saying, 'The Lord's done it! I knelt down, and there it was right across the altar: "Ave Maria."'

Tom O'Connor

When he asked me to marry him, it was like being asked if I wanted brown sauce on my sausage and egg sarnie. How could I say no? Some things just go together.

Becky Granger, *Coronation Street*

I wanted you to be the first to know: Ernest and I have blighted our trough.

Nelly Pledge, *Nearest and Dearest*

Eighteen thousand quid, that's how much the average wedding costs. That's *everything* out of the Argos catalogue... My advice: marry a Buddhist. They always want to get married under a tree. 'No problem, love. Oak or larch? It's *your* big day.'

Jeff Green

—Would you like to get married in a pub?
—Not during opening hours. It'd be a waste of good supping time.

Pat Partington and Carter Brandon, *I Didn't Know You Cared*

I hate weddings. When I go to weddings, they all say, 'You'll be next!' What I do now is, when I go to funerals, I say to the relatives, 'You'll be next!' That shuts 'em up.

Paul O'Grady

65

You can't come to my wedding, Granville, who'll look after the shop? I'll tell you what I'll do: I'll bring you back a piece o' bridesmaid.

Arkwright, *Open All Hours*

Her two bridesmaids were large ladies and would no doubt have been an asset as prop forwards for Wigan. Both were heavily muscular. One had a fake moustache and a duelling scar.

Les Dawson

My wedding dress is gonna make Liberace look like a librarian!

Becky Granger, *Coronation Street*

On the morning of the wedding, she was in a complete panic. She said, 'Something old, something new – I've got nothing borrowed and blue!' I said, 'You've got a mortgage and varicose veins, will that do?'

Victoria Wood

—What is your proudest moment?
—Marrying the most beautiful girl in the world – well, in Chester, anyway.

Reporter and John Prescott

A young woman got married at Chester,
Her mother she kissed and she blessed her.
Says she, 'You're in luck,
He's a stunning good fuck,
For I've had him myself down in Leicester.'

Anon, printed in *The Pearl* magazine, 1879

—My Uncle Hitchcock were struck by lightning at my wedding. He were doing someone a favour: he were wearing a new set of false teeth in for a neighbour, stainless-steel, they were. The bridal Humber drew up outside the church and when I emerged, my Uncle Hitchcock took one look at me, burst into a grin, and a bolt of lightning struck his dentures. Killed him stone dead!
—Fancy! That's what comes of having a sense of humour, isn't it?

Pat and Annie Brandon, *I Didn't Know You Cared*

The room where they held the reception had all the intimacy of Lenin's Tomb on half day closing... Cheap sherry was served in cracked tumblers. God knows who trod the grapes for the tepid brew, but in my glass I found a Spanish corn plaster.

Les Dawson

What a bunch of losers. It's like 'Deliverance' in evening wear.

Sadie King, *Emmerdale*

Auntie Dot from Cockermouth ate a raffia drinks coaster. She thought it was a high-fibre biscuit. She had to be held back from moving down the table and buttering two more.

Jean, *Dinnerladies*

After t'buffet, everyone's a bit pissed. DJ puts on 'Grease' megamix – 'Music Man' – Black Lace, 'Come on Eileen' – Jive Bunny. Uncle Knobhead, he's up, he's got his brand-new cream slip-ons on, his wife's got a beehive and a face like a smacked arse. They hate each other's guts but they both love jiving.

Peter Kay

67

The dreary night rolled on. The mother-in-law got drunk and stood on a chair singing all the songs she'd learned as a storm-trooper.

Les Dawson

Johnny Vegas sold his wedding pictures to *Viz*, the scatological adult magazine, for £1. The bride's grandmother was surprised to see the photographs next to a cartoon of a man with large testicles.

The Sunday Times

At 11 o'clock the happy couple left for their honeymoon in Bridlington. I thought it was a strange conjugal venue, Bridlington, 'specially since it was November, but as Agatha-Louise explained, they'd have no trouble getting deckchairs.

Les Dawson

I remember when Andy and I moved into our first house just after were married. He lovingly carried a crate of beer over the threshold.

Flo Capp

I carried her over the threshold. I remember it well: I had to make three journeys.

Peter Goodwright, *The Ken Dodd Show*

Lie Back And Think Of Grimsby: Sex

My wife is great in bed. Until I fucking get in.

Roy 'Chubby' Brown

Muck, muck, mucky mcmuck!

Ada Shufflebottom, aka Les Dawson

It's not the kind of girl I am – especially before tea.

Susie Dean, *The Good Companions*

I can't bear goaty intellectuals who think you ought to sleep with them because they are clever. There is nothing more attractive than a man who is not a New Man.

Jilly Cooper

I can't stand these New Men sitting talking about classical music and eating lettuce. I want me vest ripping off and shagging on a landing.

Lily Savage, aka Paul O'Grady

When we were teenagers, there was a church nearby, and I used to go bell-ringing once a week, to meet boys. But it's not a great preparation for a mutually fulfilling sex life, bell-ringing. All that tugging – it's not good. The first proper boyfriend I had, I nearly killed him – sorry! He didn't mind that so much as being expected to do it in a circle with seven other people.

Victoria Wood

Sex is a waste of batteries.

Morrissey

Do remember that girls like it, too.

John Peel

The only time a bloke feels like doing it twice is just before he's done it once.

Dave Spikey

I'm not from Bangkok, the sex capital of the world; I'm from Greater Manchester, the chip capital of the world, which is why all the sex shows are in Bangkok and all the chip shops are in Greater Manchester... If all the sex shows were in Greater Manchester, they would just be girls with their coats on with a chip pan going, 'Because I'm not in the mood, now leave it!'

Victoria Wood

—Prostitutes in Amsterdam are dead filthy, this one I went to, she made me wash my old man in the sink.
—What, you took your dad?

Max Bygraves and Paddy O'Shea, *Phoenix Nights*

If you're financially destitute and you've got a piece of glass shaped like a car window are you allowed to just stand there and watch?

Johnny Vegas, on dogging

I had a really horrible experience with sex that put me off for the rest of my life: I actually saw my face as I was having an orgasm. It was bloody horrible... Never ever again. It wasn't in a mirror. It was in a shop-window.

Jeff Green

[*trying to suppress an erection*] Nicholas Witchell... Nicholas Witchell... Nicholas Witchell...

Roland, *Paul and Pauline Calf's Video Diaries*

—Eh, Dolly, an unexpected day off! Shall we pick up a couple of executives at the Midland Hotel, and have an orgy?
—We could do. I might just pop home and dip me nets.

Jean and Dolly, *Dinnerladies*

I can never really believe wife-swapping actually goes on... I can't imagine an orgy going on in Bridlington: 'Eh, now, steady on, mind my barometer!'

Victoria Wood

If anyone kissed on television, my father would cough, rustle the newspaper and say: 'Eyes on sandals!'

Diana Rigg

I do not give blow jobs. Why not? Because I find it really off-putting, seeing a grown man look that pathetically grateful.

Jenny Eclair

You know the worst thing about oral sex? The view.

Maureen Lipman

He was such a caring lover, so sensitive to a woman's needs. He let me go on top so I could keep an eye on the baby.

Pauline Calf, aka Steve Coogan

We were in bed all last Sunday afternoon, doing it 'plumber's position' – you stop in all day and nobody comes.

Johnnie Casson

71

Safe sex is very important. Take precautions. Put your fag out. Move your cans where they won't get knocked over.

Paul Calf, aka Steve Coogan

You've never practised safe sex in your life. You've picked up more dirt than a JCB in your time.

Louise Brooks, *Two Pints of Lager and a Packet of Crisps*

Of course I believe in safe sex – I've got a handrail around the bed.

Ken Dodd

We haven't got much of a sex life nowadays. In fact we just lie in bed and fart at each other.

Johnnie Casson

I will never need Viagra. I am a rampant fellow.

Brian Blessed

I said to the wife, 'Have you made any New Year's resolutions?' She said, 'I'm giving up sex.' I said, 'Eh? You gave that up two years ago.' She said, 'With *you*.'

Roy 'Chubby' Brown

I saw the goat the next day – it did not seem too upset, but it is difficult to tell.

Detective Inspector Dave Crinnion, after passengers on the
Hull to Bridlington train witnessed a man having sex with the grazing
animal as the train stopped at signals

Reader, I Married Him: Marriage

I've been married now for fifteen years, on and off.

John Bishop

You've got to get married, haven't you? You can't go through life being happy.

Colin Crompton

Look at that couple: they're both aged beyond their years, they both look as miserable as sin, they both loathe going out with each other and drinking in t'same pub – if that's not proof of t'perfect marriage I don't know what is.

Uncle Mort, *I Didn't Know You Cared*

I don't think I could ever get up in church and vow to stand by a man for the rest of my life. I think of marriage as a bit like a sheep being branded.

Jane Horrocks

Every day I meet lots of beautiful women who I would marry immediately – but only for a couple of hours. I'm just not the marrying type.

Sir Jimmy Savile

Single Men: Get a glimpse of married life by taping 'Woman's Hour' on Radio 4, then playing it back at a higher volume than the TV while trying to watch something on Discovery 'Wings'.

Top tip, *Viz* magazine

So, you're an unmarried mother and you live in Essex. Couldn't you find a footballer or a bank robber?

Anne Robinson, to a contestant on *The Weakest Link*

—Do you know who I'd have married, if your Auntie Edna hadn't stuck her oar in through our nuptuals?
—No, who?
—Zelda Fitzgerald.
—Who's she?
—I don't know. It's just a name what's stuck with me since the day I had my first boil lanced.
—It's a grand name. Very redolent.
—So was my boil.

Uncle Mort and Carter Brandon, *Uncle Mort's South Country*

It wasn't an arranged marriage, more a deranged marriage.

Liam Gallagher, on marriage to Patsy Kensit (F)

—What d'you keep looking at me for?
—I'm yer 'usband – I'm entitled to look at yer.
—Well, yer can pack it in as quick as yer like...I 'aven't spent 40 years building up a relationship on *not* looking at each other for you to start now! It's very unsettling.

Nora and Wally Batty, *Last of the Summer Wine*

Are you going to cut that grass, or are you waiting till it comes in the hall?

Wife, to husband, *The Al Read Show*

Avoid endless arguments with your wife about leaving the toilet seat down by simply pissing in the sink.

Top tip, *Viz* magazine

Marriage is like the Middle East – there's no solution.

Shirley Valentine, *Shirley Valentine*

A fella said to his mate, 'I've had a lot of bad luck. I wouldn't get married again – I've been married twice.' His mate said, 'Why?' The fella said, 'Well, my first wife died eating poison mushrooms.' His mate said, 'What about your second wife?' The fella said, 'Fractured skull.' His mate said, 'How was that?' The fella said, 'She wouldn't eat her mushrooms.'

Bernard Manning

Playing Away: Infidelity

—What would you do if you found a man in bed with your wife?
—I'd kick his dog and break his white stick!

Ernie Wise and Eric Morecambe

My wife's too domineering. I caught her sucking the milkman's cock and she made me promise not to tell the window cleaner.

Roy 'Chubby' Brown

One husband said he could always tell when his wife was having an affair because the poetry books were suddenly at the horizontal on top of the shelves.

Jilly Cooper

—If we was married and I ran off with a fancy man, what would you do?
—I don't know. I s'pose I'd go back to wearing me vest in bed again.

Pat Partington and Carter Brandon, *I Didn't Know You Cared*

[*reading the headline in a newspaper*] Listen to this: 'Vicar's wife accuses cook of ding-dong in Belfry. Discarded underclothing points to vicar's infidelity.' Poor old vicar – they found his vest in her pantry and her pants in his vestry.

Arkwright, *Open All Hours*

Apparently she came home from work unexpectedly one morning and found him in bed with the milkman. Honest to God, the milkman! But from that day forward I've noticed she never takes milk in her tea.

Shirley Valentine, *Shirley Valentine*

Separation and Divorce

So, I'm bone idle, am I? That's it, Flo! Pack me bags – I'm leaving!

Andy Capp

Later he went to his home, packed some things and went. He said goodbye, made a short explanation to the dog and left.

Judge, during an actual divorce hearing in Yorkshire

In Britain, two out of three marriages end in divorce. The other one ends in murder.

Jeff Green

—I think she overreacts. She told him she wanted a divorce that time just because she caught him flirting with a couple of nurses.
—She was giving birth at the time.

Joe and Tanya, *Early Doors*

After my divorce was a terribly bitter time... I used to go to jumble sales and spend three old pennies on a whole pile of old china; cups, saucers, plates, anything, and then go home and throw them at the wall. When I look back I think that was healthy.

Liz Smith

Getting divorced isn't like a bereavement at all, because if he'd died, I'd have had me mortgage paid. And I could've danced on his grave.

Sarah Millican

—D'you miss your husband?
—Mmm, I miss the company. I'm not cut out for being on my own. If I say something like, 'I'm a fool! I've left those tomatoes on the back-seat,' it's just nice if there's someone there going, "Ave you?'

Philippa and Jean, *Dinnerladies*

—Why aren't you married any more, Mr Sharif?
—One morning, my wife and I woke up in bed and found it was no longer exciting. Being civilized people, we parted.
—Fancy. Miss Dors, can you imagine anything worse than being in bed with Omar Sharif and finding it's not exciting any more?
—Yes. Being in bed with you and finding it was.

Russell Harty, Omar Sharif (F) and Diana Dors (F), *The Russell Harty Show*

Nearest and Dearest: Family

I've realised that I am one of those lucky people who received a double blessing when I was born: first to grow up in the North of England, and second, to have had two of the best and wisest parents in the world.

Thora Hird

My childhood was just like the Waltons but without the sawmill.

Johnny Vegas

—Mum, the Boswells are here.
—Oh, good, there's nothing decent on television tonight.

Sandra and Mrs Hutchinson, *The Liver Birds*

I come from a family of fourteen. My father didn't lie in bed all day doing nowt.

Scarlet O'Hara

We were the biggest family in the street. When we all bent down in the playpen on bath-night, it were like a crate of peaches.

Ada Shufflebottom, aka Les Dawson

I've got a brother, our Archie. I hate him. In fact, the only reason I speak to him is because you never know when you might need a kidney.

Lily Savage, aka Paul O'Grady

Sure I love Liam, but not as much as I love Pot Noodles.

Noel Gallagher

My brother, Geoff, is long-suffering. In fact, at my 50th birthday party, he gave a speech entitled 'Reflections of the Brother of an Only Child'.

Maureen Lipman

She's such a cow...but she's *our* cow, and we've got to support her.

Blanche Hunt, on her granddaughter, Tracy Barlow, *Coronation Street*

—I met Mum in the market this morning. She hasn't been herself lately.
—Yes, I've noticed the improvement.

Flo and Andy Capp

The mother-in-law thinks I'm effeminate. Not that I mind, because, beside her, I am.

Les Dawson

I used to have a mother-in-law who lived in France – which is not as far away as you think.

John Bishop

I invited this man round for dinner. Halfway through the meal he said, 'I don't like your mother-in-law.' So I said, 'Leave her on the side of the plate and just eat the chips and peas.'

Charlie Williams

My Nan used to say: 'Here's £5 – don't tell your mother.' I'd say: 'Why not?' She'd say: 'It's hers.'

Lee Mack

What a wonderful day it is for grandad-baiting! Stick a rabbit and a ferret in his trousers and see how long it is before his eyes cross.

Ken Dodd

Don't Some Mothers 'Ave 'Em: **Children**

We have lots of rows about the whole baby thing. I wanted to have a baby for about five years – but my wife wants to keep it for ever.

Lee Mack

—What's that?
—It's a turkey baster.
—What am I supposed to do, lie back and think of Bernard Matthews?

Max Farnham and Jacqui Dixon, *Brookside*

—In my family, a man has only to look at a woman and she's pregnant.
—That's because you're all so cock-eyed.

Denny and Rita, *Educating Rita*

—Have you any idea what I'm going through?
—What *you're* going through? I'm going to be a father and I'm only 39.
—You're from up north, you should be a *grandfather* by now.

Tim (F) and Lee, *Not Going Out*

Tommy Higgins reckons as 'ow 'eatin' black puddings on an empty stomach is one thing that'll bring it on. That's why they call it t'pudding club.

George Fairchild, *Brass*

The other day I was in the doctor's, and I was reading 'Cosmopolitan'. ... They had a 'top ten' list of 'The Most Painful Things in Life That Women Have to Endure'. I thought, well, number one's got to be: 'Childbirth'. No, that was number two. Number one was: 'Having your nipples clamped'. I thought, no, 'Having them towed away' has got to be worse.

Dave Spikey

The wife of a mad-keen Yorkshire cricket fan was in the maternity hospital. Her husband, anxious not to miss a moment of the Roses match, was at home watching TV. His only contact with his wife was by phone. When bad light stopped play for a few moments, he rang the hospital to find out how she was getting on. 'She's had the baby,' said the ward sister, 'but there might be another on the way. Can you ring back in half an hour?' He went back to the TV and half an hour later, during the tea interval, he called again. 'Sorry, but there's another on the way!' said the sister. 'Can you ring back in another half an hour?' The man went back to the match. Half an hour later, he picked up the phone to call the hospital again. But, in his haste, he accidentally called the Test score phone line instead. 'Can you tell me how my wife's doing?' he said to the recorded message. 'It's 125 all out,' came the reply, 'and the last one was a duck.'

Bill Shipton

It was easier than having a tattoo.

Noel Gallagher, on the birth of Liam and Nicole Appleton's son, Gene

Since my baby shoved her great fat head out, my vagina's gone like a woolly in the wash – it's all baggy round the neck. I don't use tampons any more, I just roll up the duvet – although they're a bugger to flush away.

Jenny Eclair

When I had my daughter, I had to have stitches. I did ask them to put a couple of extra ones in, as a special treat for me husband, really. He said it really improved things. He said before that it was like waving a stick in the Albert Hall.

Pauline Calf, aka Steve Coogan

—Did someone drop you on your head when you were a baby?
—No.
—They fuckin' should 'ave.

Pauline Calf, aka Steve Coogan, and Gormless Friend

I've only got one child. People say, 'Won't she be lonely?' I say, 'No, she's got Sky Plus.'

Jenny Eclair

—If you didn't whistle, you wouldn't know where to wipe your arse, you daft bastard.
—Mum, she called me a bastard!
—Well, you are one, love.

Pauline, Paul and Mrs Calf, aka Steve Coogan and Sandra Gough

I feel a bit sorry for kids today. They don't get to hang around on the corner or go up on the moor drinking cider. They have to be in by 10pm.

Mark E. Smith

As a child, my main talents were falling out of trees, digging holes and setting fire to my coat.

Ken Dodd

I had a happy childhood. We were poor, but we were shoplifters.

Lily Savage, aka Paul O'Grady

I got kicked out of the Scouts for eating a brownie.

Ross Noble

When you do 'Pass the Parcel' now, when you make up the parcel, you have to put a little prize in each layer, so each child who unwraps a layer gets a little prize to take home. There was none of that when I was little. You were lucky if you got one when you got to the end. You'd unwrap the last thing and go, 'There's nothing in it, Mrs Pickering.' 'No, that's life, that is, think on!'

Victoria Wood

As children, my brother and I were frequently snapped out of sulks by being told we had 'a face like a spare dinner that's fallen on a mucky rug'.

Wendy Holden

Kids today get bored dead easily. It winds me up. When I was a kid, a dead bumblebee would give me two weeks of fun. I'd know where it was on the street; I'd even have a stick to poke it.

Mick Ferry

All my teenage daughter can do is watch television, and sometimes even that's too much for her. Last night she said to me, 'Mum, I'm tired. Will you watch "Hollyoaks" for me?'

Jenny Eclair

Like its politicians and its war, society has the teenagers it deserves.

J.B. Priestley

There are so many more important things to do than have children. My experience of having children is that they are individuals who are nothing to do with you at all. They might as well be anybody's children.

Vivienne Westwood

I don't regret not having children. It's a daily celebration that I haven't had them because I know I would hurl them all off the balcony.

Sir Jimmy Savile

Can You Hear Me, Mother? Mother

For a while, I was the perfect mother. Then the Pethidine wore off.

Jenny Eclair

There's no such thing as a perfect mother. A mother's place is in the wrong.

Anne Robinson

I always believed that my daughter should be brought up the same way as I was – so my mother had her for six days a week.

Pauline Daniels

I was brought up by me mam. Why she couldn't give birth the normal way still remains a mystery.

Roy 'Chubby' Brown

You're not a mother until you've had nits.

Coleen Nolan

My mother's beyond stoic. She had polio and only has one kidney. She was born without sentiment – she cut up her wedding dress and turned it into a lampshade.

Jenny Eclair

My mother never let me get away with anything. I wasn't allowed to watch daytime television, she never gave me lift to school, and she didn't believe in period-pains.

Jenny Eclair

I was fine up to the age of 11, but then I started putting on weight. I brought my last girlfriend home to see my parents and I was telling her how it all started going wrong when I was 11. My mum then said: 'You mustn't say things like that – you were 8 when things started to go wrong.'

Johnny Vegas

If Amy Winehouse had a northern mother, she wouldn't be injecting heroin between her toes. She'd be sat at the table, elbows off, eating a meat 'n' potato pie.

Jenny Eclair

Robert Maxwell was just like my mother. I'm not saying she would have thieved people's pensions, but he had a method of doing business like a benign dictator that to me seemed very normal.

Anne Robinson

My mother would say, 'Valerie, what on earth do you think you are doing? We do not sit down to iron.'

Valerie Johnson

Mam likes the quiet life. When the money came in, well, that's obviously a new house? No. She's still at the council house we moved to when she left me dad. We bought it. All she wanted was a new garden gate because the old one creaked.

Noel Gallagher

Mums are murder when you're having a family meal: 'Have you got enough?' 'D'you want more potatoes?' 'Is that hot enough?' 'Are you sure it's cooked through?' 'D'you want more vegetables?' 'We've got enough, Mum, you get yours.' But mums don't eat. Mums come in with the tiniest portion of food. 'Is that all you're 'aving, Mum?' 'I had a Ryvita yesterday.'

Peter Kay

The thought of Sunday lunch at home with the family. There was my mother, 19 stones of menopause, wielding an electric carving knife. OK, she was carving a chicken, but she was looking at me.

Jenny Eclair

My mum taught me how to bounce back from setbacks – she has a wonderful Northern expression: 'Spit on your hands and take a fresh hold.'

Lesley Garrett

My mam'd still be dressing me if I let her.

Joe, *Early Doors*

Things I won't miss about not living with me mum any more: I won't miss her shaving her legs with my Mach 3, but I will miss her being able to turn over a cauliflower cheese grill with the palm of her hand.

Peter Kay

Wives change but your mother will always be your mother.

Fred Dibnah, on changing the name of his traction engine from
'Alison' to 'Betsy' after separating from his wife

When my mum gets a little embarrassing at a party, my dad says to her: 'Say goodnight, mother of five.' She replies: 'Goodnight, father of four!'

Ted Robbins

—She must've been a very special woman, your mother.
—No, she was just me mam.

Mrs Wilkinson and Billy Elliot, *Billy Elliot*

Father

My dad was a football fanatic and he worked in a sweet factory. What else does a boy need?

Brian Clough

Dads are amazing. They can do stuff that nobody's ever taught them, like changing a plug with a butter knife. That's in no DIY manual is it?

Jason Manford

He's the funniest man in the world, my dad. Kind of bloke that could read out a telephone directory and it'd be funny. I mean, to be fair, he used to do it with his cock out.

Lee Mack

My dad taught me to ride a bike by chasing after me with an axe and shouting, 'Come here, you bastard!'

Boothby Graffoe

You see dads nowadays, always hanging around their kids. It's ridiculous. It's more about them than the kids, their ideas. My dad worked all day and he'd be out all night.

Mark E.Smith, *Renegade*

I remember ringing my dad to tell him I'd got a third for my degree: 'Dad, I got the lowest mark in the whole year. I'm really sorry. I feel I've let you down.' My dad said: 'You haven't let me down, son. I never thought you'd pass in the first place.'

Johnny Vegas

My father gave me this advice: 'Save a pound if you earn two pounds, never eat fish on Mondays, and never play snooker with a left-handed Welsh miner.'

Ted Ray

My dad gave me only one piece of advice. He said, 'Son, you can do anything you like so long as you never support Everton.'

Des Merton

Dad's kindness and sentimentality...extended to inanimate objects. He kept 36 years' worth of Mum's shopping lists, a whole box of Kid Jensen's postcards and all of the used diabetic needles that he didn't offer as gifts. His collection of £2 coins, which he gathered lovingly, will be paying for his gravestone.

> William, Alexandra, Tom and Florence on their dad, John Peel,
> read out at his memorial service

My father's last words to me before he died were: 'Do what you want, I never did.'

> George Melly

'Ome Sweet 'Ome

Half of the people on my estate dream of owning their own homes. The other half dream of breaking into them when they get them.

> Roy 'Chubby' Brown

I'd never stone clad my house. It'd look like a white filling in a mouth full of rotten teeth.

> Judee Levinson, *The League of Gentlemen*

I mean, 'ere's me, I've got on, and yet I 'ave to look out of my window at a lot of hovels, whereas you lot in yer hovels 'ave the undeserved pleasure of looking out at my nice house. Often rankles does that.

> Bradley Hardacre, *Brass*

We're going to Mobberley. We've found a house we like. It's got underfloor heating. That'll cut down on our slipper bill.

> Dolly, *Dinnerladies*

I like old houses, houses with old carpets and damp bedrooms what discourage visitors.

Les Brandon, *I Didn't Know You Cared*

The house was so damp the mice were strangled by an octopus.

Les Dawson

The condescension was running down the walls.

Nelly Pledge, *Nearest and Dearest*

You get no sun on this side at all. What you could really do with is your house turning right round.

Al Read

—I've got some wallpaper to show you. [*opens roll*] Get that on this wall, it'll go down a treat.
—Oh, that's 'orrible!
—But that's what they're all 'avin'. They go mad for that in London.
—Yeah, well, we haven't gone mad up 'ere yet.

Eddie Yates and Hilda Ogden, *Coronation Street*

Buy a tin of blood-red paint. Take it home and write on the wall with the paint, 'I WILL KILL AGAIN!' Wait for it to dry, then put your wallpaper up. You never actually get to see the punchline to that little practical joke, but you do get a lovely warm feeling in five years' time when you hand the keys over.

Chris Addison

I've come into this 'ouse, more times than I care to remember, cold, wet, tired out, not a penny in me purse, and the sight o' them ducks and that murial, well, they've kept me away from the gas tap an' that's a fact.

Hilda Ogden, *Coronation Street*

—Ooh, Denise, is this the new sofa?
—Yeah. It's flame-retarded.

Barbara Royle and Denise Best, *The Royle Family*

Owners of smoke alarms – where's your sense of adventure?

Top tip, *Viz* magazine

Get Off Me Steps! **Housework**

Northern women's lives are slung between three poles: dirt, disease and the lavatory.

Alan Bennett

Monday was washday, Tuesday was ironing. Wednesday and Thursday were cleaning. Friday was baking. Saturday was shopping and Sunday we went out for a walk.

Alan Titchmarsh, *Nobbut a Lad*

What a day! Hoovering, dusting, polishing – how's a man supposed to nap when his wife's doing all that?

Andy Capp

I'm married to a scruffy one. Every time you go to have a pee in the sink, it's full of dishes.

Jackie Hamilton

—My mother was spotless. You could eat your grub off the floor in our house.
—Well you had to. You had no furniture.

Billy Martin and Bobby Hooper

How many men does it take to change a toilet roll? Nobody knows. It's never been tried.

Ken Dodd

DIY

Last Bank Holiday, my wife said, 'You've been promising to put some of those shelves up in the alcove.' I said, 'I know you, you'll want 'em straight and everything.' So I go to the library for a DIY book. I actually went into the library and said to the girl, ''Scuse me, love, 'ave you any books on shelves?'

Dave Spikey

You great useless futtock! If you want anything doin' round 'ere, don't ask a man! You're all the same! If you don't have to take your trousers off to do it, you're just not interested.

Ivy, *Last of the Summer Wine*

I keep two small screwdrivers in my kitchen to repair domestic appliances which my husband, who has 34 screwdrivers in his toolbox, borrows. Can a man ever have too many screwdrivers?

Paddie Breeze

If you have dry rot, it's best to do this job sitting down.

Ken Dodd

How many birds does it take to change a lightbulb? Two. One to run around screaming, 'What do I do?' and the other to shag the electrician.

DCI Gene Hunt, Ashes To Ashes

Heard about the glazier who repaired 146 windows before realising he had cracked glasses?

Ken Dodd

Sport and Recreation

Come On. No, Wait! Get Back... Sorry! Cricket

I should challenge the Englishness of any man who could walk down a country lane, come unexpectedly on a cricket match, and not lean over the fence and watch for a while.

Neville Cardus

[*gazing at a model of the cricket pavilion at Bramall Lane*] By God, that's a sight for sore eyes. The memories it brings back. Miller and Lindwall in full flood. Hutton stroking the ball majestically through the covers. Freddie Trueman knocking the stuffing out of them bastards from Lancashire. Aye, many's the good kip I've had in there.

Uncle Mort, Uncle Mort's North Country

Some are born with silver spoons in their mouths. I was born in Pudsey. You can't be luckier than that if you want to play cricket.

Ray Illingworth

In an England cricket eleven, the flesh may be of the South, but the bone is of the North, and the backbone is Yorkshire.

Len Hutton

He may be good enough for England, but not for Yorkshire.

Brian Sellers, after Yorkshire sacked Johnny Wardle

The most important thing in my life was when I received my Yorkshire cap back in 1955. As we always said – Fred, myself, Close...getting your Yorkshire cap probably meant more to you at that time than getting your England cap.

Ray Illingworth, *The Corridor of Uncertainty*

David Bairstow personifies the best virtues of Yorkshireness – he doesn't give a toss for his reputation, fights back when cornered and doesn't even contemplate defeat.

Michael Parkinson

N.W.D. Yardley, captain of Yorkshire and England, played in flannels so cream that they were almost khaki. I never saw a grass stain on elbow or knee. In those days, sliding and diving fielders were virtually unknown. When in 1949 a New Zealander called Brunton Smith flung himself full-length to prevent a Yorkshire boundary, the Bramall Lane crowd booed his unsporting behaviour.

Roy Hattersley

We shake hands on t'first morning and say, 'How do.' Then we say nowt for three days but, 'Howzat.'

Roy Kilner, on Roses matches during the 1920s

In cricket, brute strength and ignorance can go a long way.

Len Hutton

Cricket is 50 per cent in the head, 50 per cent in the heart and bugger technique.

Ray Illingworth

Paul Harris is a buffet bowler: you just help yourself.

Geoffrey Boycott

A snick by Jack Hobbs is a sort of disturbance of cosmic orderliness.

Neville Cardus

You can't have 11 Darren Goughs on your side – it would drive you nuts. It would be like having 11 Phil Tufnells.

Darren Gough

A true batsman should in most of his strokes tell the truth about himself.

Neville Cardus

What you get from Nasser Hussain is honesty. There aren't many captains who look you in the eye and tell you you're a tosser.

Darren Gough

Dickie Bird arrived on earth from the Planet Looney to become the best and fairest of all umpires. Great bloke, completely bonkers.

Ian Botham

Cricket's my wife.

Dickie Bird

I suppose if you don't play in gloom up here, you never play at all.

Alan Knott (F), on Old Trafford

I refused to play cricket – it was dull... standing in front of a great yob who's hurling a rock at you, interspersed with enormous periods of standing around suffering from hay fever.

Jeremy Clarkson

Before he gathered together 20 runs, a newly-married couple could have left Heathrow and arrived in Lisbon, there to enjoy a honeymoon. By the time Bailey had congealed 50, this happily wedded pair could easily have settled down in a semi-detached house in Surbiton; and by the time his innings had gone to its close they conceivably might have been divorced.

Neville Cardus, on a slow innings by Trevor Bailey (F)

My auntie could have caught that in her pinny.

Geoffrey Boycott

Just when he thought it couldn't get much worse, England cricket captain Mike Atherton's girl has dumped him. Just as well she hasn't give him her heart. He would only have dropped it.

The Sun

Concentration is sometimes mistaken for grumpiness.

Mike Atherton

Of the three Yorkshiremen who have scored 100 hundreds, the most beautiful player, by far, was Hutton. The man to play an innings for your life was Sutcliffe. The man to play an innings for his own life is Boycott.

Alan Gibson

—You'd want Geoffrey Boycott to bat for your life.
—It would either be a long life or a slow death.

Henry Blofeld (F) and Alec Stewart (F)

You'll never die of a stroke, Boycott.

Fred Trueman

In his century at Headingley, Boycott touched the ankle of his right foot 40 times each hour. He took off his cap and wiped his brow 364 times. He played 466 balls. He marks his guard twice every time he gets down to the business end, one at the usual mark, the other inside his crease.

Jack Fingleton (F)

[In two television documentaries] we were invited to reassess two great northern monsters, in 'Myra: The Making Of A Monster' on Five, and 'The Real Geoff Boycott' on Channel 4. A key difference between the two programmes was that obviously it was easier to find people prepared to speak up for Myra Hindley than it was to find anyone with much of a good word for Boycs. Hindley, after all, only participated in some of the grisliest murders of the 20th century, whereas Geoffrey ran out Derek Randall at Trent Bridge.

Martin Kelner

'The Real Geoff Boycott' on Channel 4 implied that 'the powerful
attraction exerted by this apparently charmless man' may have lain in his
discovery of a kind of Yorkshire version of tantric sex. That is, he made
love like he played cricket: slowly, methodically, but with the very real
possibility he might stay in all day.

Martin Kelner

Next bloody ball, bloody belt it, or I'll wrap your bat round your bloody
head.

Brian Close, to Geoff Boycott, during the Gillette Cup Final, 1965

Ian Botham represents everything that's the best in Britain. He's Biggles,
the VC, El Alamein, the tank commander. He's everything. I mean how
could a schoolboy not want to be like Ian Botham?

Tim Hudson, his agent

Ian Botham is definitely every woman's piece of rough...in the long, long
grass...by the lake...under a full moon.

Tim Hudson, his agent

Ian Botham would make a great Aussie.

Jeff Thomson (F)

England needs to pick players who don't have skeletons in their coffins.

Ian Botham

Ian Botham's idea of team spirit and motivation was to squirt a water pistol at someone and then go and get pissed.

> Ray Illingworth, on why he wouldn't be employing Botham
> as a 'motivator' for the England team

Tha'll 'ave trouble wi' t'bugger.

> Brian Sellers, the day that Leicestershire signed Ray Illingworth

In his latter days, Jack Fingleton was a disappointed observer of the decline of attitudes, both on and off the cricket field. I think what finally polished Jack off was the news that the England team to visit Australia contained a cricketer wearing an earring.

> Michael Parkinson

On the subject of skin care, James Anderson says, 'I always use a daily moisturiser.' It's one of the great tragedies that Fred Trueman is no longer on Test Match Special, because Jonathan Agnew asking Fred what type of moisturiser he used in his day could have produced one of sport's truly great radio moments.

> Martin Johnson (F)

I need nine wickets from this match, and you buggers had better start drawing straws to see who I don't get.

> Fred Trueman

Don't bother shutting it, son, you won't be there long enough.

> Fred Trueman to the incoming Aussie batsman as he opened the gate
> on the way out to the middle of the pitch

—Tell me, Fred, did you ever bowl a ball that merely went straight?
—Aye, I did – and it went straight through like a stream of piss and flattened all three.

Teammate and Fred Trueman

—In your prime, were you as quick as Denis Lillee?
—I'm quicker than him now – with my coat on.

Fan and Fred Trueman, 1996

I'd have looked even faster in colour.

Fred Trueman, after watching black and white footage of himself bowling

I had asked the publishers to call my biography 'T'Definitive Volume on T'Finest Fast Bowler That Ever Drew Breath'. But the silly buggers just intend to call it 'Fred'.

Fred Trueman

A spectator at a Roses match politely applauded a cover drive and was then turned on by a man in cap and overcoat. 'Are you from Yorkshire?' 'Er, no.' 'Lancashire?' 'Er, no.' 'Then shut tha' bloody mouth.'

Laurie Taylor

Yorkshire were 232 all out. Hutton ill. No! I'm sorry, Hutton 111.

John Snagge (F)

In those days cricket often seemed to me to be an occupation of heroes. One man took guard against eleven... Batsmen who backed away to leg were assumed to be afraid of fast bowling. If, when I watched Len

Hutton open the batting for Yorkshire, someone had predicted that, one day, batsmen would wear chest protectors, arm-guards and visored helmets, I would have assumed that they had read too much science fiction.

Roy Hattersley

Drink is a serious problem, particularly on cricket tours.... nothing yet devised by man is worse for a sick hangover than a day's cricket in the summer sun.

Michael Parkinson

Well, your lordships, Ah can only say Ah'm sorry, reight sorry... But it strikes me as bein' like this... if Ah can go down to Lord's and get drunk and mek a century 'fore lunch, then Ah think it ud pay t'Notts Committee to ge mi drunk afore every match.

Bill Barnes, up before the Nottingham Committee after scoring a century whilst tipsy, as reported by Neville Cardus

That means I can drive a flock of sheep through the town centre, drink for free in no less than 64 pubs and get a lift home with the police when I become inebriated – what more could you want?

Andrew 'Freddie' Flintoff on being given the freedom of Preston, his home town

I would die tomorrow if I could have five more years to play cricket for Yorkshire and England.

Geoff Boycott

Boxing

I'm not name-dropping, but I was talking to Frank Bruno the other day. I went, 'You big useless bastard! You big useless thick cunt!' I don't know what he said cos I put the phone down on him.

Roy 'Chubby' Brown

I was a pretty handy fighter in my youth. I could lick any man with one hand. Unfortunately, I could never find anyone with one hand who wanted a fight.

Eric Morecambe

We might look on Ricky Hatton's old-school diet of sausage and chips with the sort of alarm you might expect to see on the face of a museum curator who has just watched Heurelho Gomes pick up a Ming vase... His new trainer, Floyd Mayweather Sr, has so altered the Mancunian's diet that these days they can get him to put his gumshield in without having to coat it in batter first.

Harry Pearson

Darts: Sid Waddell On The Oche

Jocky Wilson...what an athlete!

He's majestic, just like that great big fat bloke singing Nessun Dorma.

He's playing out of his pie crust.

The atmosphere is so tense, if Elvis walked in with a portion of chips, you could hear the vinegar sizzle on them.

Bristow reasons ... Bristow quickens ... Aaahhhhh, Bristow.

When Alexander of Macedonia was 33 he cried salt tears because there were no more worlds to conquer. Bristow is only 27.

Look at the man go, it's like trying to stop a water buffalo with a pea-shooter.

That was like throwing three pickled onions into a thimble!

Steve Beaton, he's not Adonis, he's *The*-Donis.

Just when he's had your meat and two veg, he comes back and nicks yer puddin'!

Not even Harry Houdini covered in rubbing oil could have got out of that one!

Dennis Priestley's darts are going into the 60 at more angles than Hypotenuse ever dreamed of.

He's as happy as a polar bear in a sauna.

This lad has more checkouts than Tesco's.

We couldn't have more excitement if Elvis walked in and asked for a chip sandwich.

Tony Brown attacks his opponents the same way Desperate Dan attacks cow pie.

Fordham is sweating like a hippo in a power shower.

That's the greatest comeback since Lazarus.

Up And Under: Rugby

When I say rugby of course I mean rugby league, not the other sort
wherein wheezing off-duty policemen, solicitors and dentists bite each
other's noses off, watched by retired headmasters in driving gloves.

Stuart Maconie, *Cider With Roadies*

—What's the difference between rugby league and rugby union?
—Two less idiots.

Bob Mills

A friend of mine once said, perceptively, that rugby union has but one
saving grace, namely that it's always nice to see coppers getting knocked
about a bit on their day off.

Stuart Maconie, *Cider With Roadies*

Rugby league is war without the frills.

Anon

In south-west Lancashire, babes don't toddle, they side-step. Queuing
women talk of 'nipping round the blindside'. Rugby league provides our
cultural adrenalin. It's a physical manifestation of our rules of life,
comradeship, honest endeavour, and a staunch, often ponderous
allegiance to fair play.

Colin Welland

Bradford is famous for sheep, but we didn't think that had quite the same
ring. When we asked on local radio for a name with Yorkshire
connotations someone suggested puddings. So it's Bulls.

Peter Deakin, on renaming Bradford Northern, the Bulls

I want to sell Rugby League to the local people. The match ball for our first game will be brought to the pitch by parachute. We also plan to have majorettes and Morris dancers. After all, this is Kent.

Paul Faires (F), chairman, Kent Invicta, now defunct

Golf

I'd rather be thought a poof than a golfer.

Jeremy Clarkson

Golf is a fascinating game. It has taken me nearly forty years to discover that I can't play it.

Ted Ray

When male golfers wiggle their feet to get their stance right they look exactly like cats preparing to pee.

Jilly Cooper

An Irishman was on a golf course for the first time. He hit the ball and it went straight into a bunker. Finally, after several attempts, he hits it out of the bunker and it goes straight into the hole. The Irishman said: 'Sod this game, I'll never get it out of there.'

Bernard Manning

—You know what your main trouble is?
—What?
—You stand too close to the ball after you've hit it.

Eric Morecambe and Ernie Wise

Golfers: empty egg boxes make ideal containers for your golf balls. Except that they're a little bit too small.

Top tip, Viz magazine

Football

I've had a terrible day. I got home from work and my house was burnt down, the wife's run away with my best mate, the two kids have pinched my car and gone to sea, and Liverpool lost. I can't understand it cos they were winning at half time.

Tom O'Connor

Cilla wants her teeth back, Cilla wants her teeth back, la, la, la, la, la, la...

Liverpool Fans, welcoming toothsome Ronaldinho to Anfield

A Liverpool supporter loves his team, follows them all over Europe. He comes down one morning, his wife says to him, 'You know something, Charlie, I think you love Liverpool more than me.' He says, 'I love *Everton* more than you.'

Mike Burton

I love Liverpool so much that if I caught one of the players in bed with my missus I'd tiptoe downstairs and make him a cup of tea.

Unidentified Koppite

It's going to be a giro cup final: Everton v. Liverpool.

Unidentified Scouser

St Anthony, Blessed Oliver Plunkett and St Theresa: Many thanks for finding lost UEFA Cup ticket.

Notice, *Liverpool Echo*

Man offers marriage to any woman with ticket for Leeds United v. Sheffield United game. Must send photograph (of ticket).

Advert, *Yorkshire Evening Post*

Some Hull City supporters have had to wait 104 years for this day...

Football commentator, Radio 5 Live

To say that these men paid their shillings to watch twenty-two hirelings kick a ball is merely to say that a violin is wood and catgut, that 'Hamlet' is so much paper and ink. For a shilling the Bruddersford United AFC offered you Conflict and Art.

J.B. Priestley

Have we got any Manchester United fans in tonight? [*Loud cheers from the audience*] 'Course we 'ave – we're in Hammersmith! Manchester United fans are like rats: you're only ever 3 metres away from one of the bastards.

Jason Manford, Man City supporter

I said to my wife that there's Man City and Man United, and she pointed out that they sound like gay clubs.

Michael McIntyre (F)

UNITED. KIDS. WIFE. IN THAT ORDER.

Banner at Arsenal v. Man Utd football match

For a ticket to the cup final I'd shag me mother-in-law.

Unidentified Manchester United Supporter

'Have you heard the news?' the shopkeeper said. 'Keegan's been killed in a freak accident. He was walking across the Tyne and the Shields Ferry hit him.'

Harry Pearson, The Far Corner

Paul Gascoigne is Tyneside's very own Renaissance Man. A man capable of breaking both leg and wind at the same time.

Jimmy Greaves (F)

I remember bumping into a coloured centre-forward then on the Newcastle books called Tony Cunningham. He had rather a bemused look. I asked him what was up and he said Paul Gascoigne had given him a present. I said there didn't seem much wrong with that. He laughed and added, 'But do I really look as if I need a week's course on a sunbed?'

Steve Howey

I asked the players who wanted to take a penalty and there was an awful smell coming from a few of them.

Mick McCarthy, on an FA Cup penalty-shoot-out

Anyone who uses the word 'quintessentially' in a half-time talk is talking crap.

Mick McCarthy, responding to a comment by Niall Quinn

I've got more points on my licence. I'm not joking.

Paul Jewell, manager of Derby County (resigned 2008)

I complain about referees as long and loud as anyone but I wouldn't have their job for a gold pig.

Mick McCarthy

Joe Mercer once observed that the trouble with modern sport is that you rarely see anyone smile on the field of play.

Michael Parkinson

—The whole pitch for the Champions League Final was flown in from Lithuania.
—I didn't know that. What? On a massive aeroplane?

John O'Farrell (F) and Lee Mack, *Have I Got News For You*

If God had wanted football to be played in the air, he wouldn't have put grass on the ground.

Brian Clough

Cristiano Ronaldo is 6 feet 2 inches, brave as a lion, strong as an ox and quick as lightning. If he was good looking you'd say he has everything.

Paul Jewell

If Steve Daly had taken 12 shots at John Lennon, he'd still be alive today.

Bernard Manning

Footballers tend not to notice or enjoy what's around them. I remember once on a tour of Italy the coach passed the Leaning Tower of Pisa. I pointed it out, only to be told, 'Shut up and deal!'

Bobby Charlton

I had a trial for Man City, but I was terrible – missed an open goal, headed it into me own net. I was absolute shite. Anyway, they offered me a place. But I was 16. I wanted to concentrate on smoking.

Paul Calf, aka Steve Coogan

—I once had a trial for Stockport County.
—Ooh, was you found guilty?

Rudyard Kettle and Louis St John, *I Didn't Know You Cared*

You can tell how well a football team's doing by the state of the footballers' wives. Second-division wives always need their roots touching up.

Mrs Merton, aka Caroline Aherne

Football was a man's game and we got stuck into it. I recall playing at Bury after a rainstorm and the pitch was a quagmire. I said to t'captain, 'If you win the toss, stick with the tide.'

Charlie Williams

His teammates nicknamed him 'Dracula' because he was no good with crosses.

Mick Miller

That was a cross! If he meant it as a shot I'll drop my trousers in Burton's window.

Mick McCarthy, on a 'freak' goal by Jan Åge Fjørtoft (F)

I was never a fancy player, but I could stop them buggers that were.

Charlie Williams

Tear 'is leg off and 'it 'im with the soggy end!

Chant from Liverpool fans

—What would you have done if you'd been Mick McCarthy and Roy Keane had spoken to you like he did?
—Oh, I'd have sent him home all right, but I'd have shot him first.

Reporter and Brian Clough

George Best, you were a sixties sensation. All that marvellous football you played and then, of course, all the booze. Did you ever think, if you hadn't done all that running round playing football, would you have been as thirsty?

Mrs Merton, aka Caroline Aherne

I walked in at night behaving like a football manager and I'd watch my three bairns sitting around thinking, 'What is it tonight?' and 'God help us if it's a bad result.'

Brian Clough

I've had enough. As soon I get home I'm gonna buy that club. I'm gonna walk in and say, 'You...fuck off; you...fuck off; you...fuck off; you...make me a cup of tea.'

Noel Gallagher, after a disappointing performance by Manchester City, in 1988

There is no way I would want to buy Manchester City. Why would I want to give every penny I have earned to some horrible little chav footballer so he can buy his wife dresses to wear at Aintree? I would rather piss it up the wall.

Noel Gallagher, 2007

It'll be nice to know that every gallon of petrol a Manchester United fan buys is going into our transfer kitty.

> Noel Gallagher, on the takeover of Manchester City by the ruling family of Abu Dhabi, the oil-rich Gulf state, 2008

Already Noel Gallagher has been quoted as saying: 'It'll be nice to know that every gallon of petrol a Manchester United fan buys is going into our kitty.' Although this line has been doing the rounds since Monday, no doubt it will be claimed as an Oasis original, a bit like their music.

> Richard Peters

Andy gets a bit depressed in the summer when there's no football on TV. Swearing at tennis isn't as satisfying.

> Flo Capp

The Gospel According to Brian Clough

Stand up straight, get your shoulders back and get your hair cut.

Young man, take your hands out of your pockets.

My philosophy has always been that if you are going to be a manager – or anything else for that matter – that you might as well be the best one there is.

They say that Rome wasn't built in a day, but I wasn't on that particular job.

You can split footballers into two categories. There were 'those who can play' and 'those who can't'. You'll be surprised how many people can't tell the difference. Some of them are managers.

I'd want them to tell me: is it the birds, is it the booze or is it the betting? Cos most of us are susceptible to one of those things. If I find out that someone likes a bet, I can watch the size of this wallet. If I find out someone likes to chase women, I can see whether his fly is undone. If someone likes a beer, I'll get close enough to smell his breath in the morning. Now that's management.

One of the worst crimes you can commit, not just in football but in life, is to ask people to deliver something they haven't got. That destroys them totally.

Some people thought me to be a bully but I never meant to be. Possibly it's the way I talk.

Say nowt. Win something. And then talk your head off.

If the BBC ran a Crap Decision of the Month competition on 'Match of the Day', I'd walk it.

I believe I have been good for football. I do not tell many lies. I am not too big a cheat. And I do not pay lip-service to influential people.

Did Yer Like Tha'? Fun

She said, 'Kitty – do you like fun?' I said, 'No, I don't. I had enough of that in 1958 when I got trapped in a lift with a Hula-Hoop salesman.'

Kitty, *Victoria Wood, As Seen on TV*

I would never, ever, do anything as vulgar as having fun.

Morrissey

What I'm out for's a good time. All the rest is propaganda.

Arthur Seaton, *Saturday Night and Sunday Morning*

Everyone over 50 should be issued every week with a wet fish in a plastic bag by the Post Office so that, whenever you see someone young and happy, you can hit them as hard as you can across the face.

Richard Griffiths

I like looking at clouds and eating cheese at the same time. I can stare at something for quite a long time.

Vic Reeves

—I thought you said you didn't like enjoyment.
—Oh, I do, provided it don't interfere with yer being miserable.

Carter Brandon and Uncle Mort, *I Didn't Know You Cared*

Gambling

'Ard lines, yer rent came in third!

Andy Capp

Winning streak? You lost £2 last week when you bet the Archbishop of Canterbury would be the next Pope.

Nelly Pledge, *Nearest and Dearest*

Don't knock Bingo. It's the only chance working-class people will ever have of owning a giant ceramic cheetah.

Johnny Vegas

—You should go to church. It's time you saw the inside of something other than the betting shop.
—At least in there you don't have to die to collect your winnings.

Cyril Blamire and William 'Compo' Simmonite, *Last of the Summer Wine*

Open All Hours: Shopping

My wife wanted a new fridge that's the size of a bungalow. So, she wanted a new fridge and cos I like sex, I said, 'Yeah.'

John Bishop

Heard about the dyslexic pervert? Went into an S&M shop and bought a nice cardigan.

John Cooper Clarke

—Can you manage the supermarket shopping, Mum?
—Good heavens, yes, dear – I've opened enough of them.

Carol Thatcher (F) and Margaret Thatcher, after leaving office

I saw this woman in the car park in Netto. She was in her car nuttin' the steering wheel; I thought she must have missed a major item on her shopping list. I looked again and saw she was, in fact, just trying to pull her seat forward.

John Shuttleworth, aka Graham Fellows

The local post office is an arena where the community meets. It is a corner shop with royal assent.

Brian Redhead

Don't touch the things. This is a local shop for local people. There's nothing in here for you.

Tubbs Tattsyrup, The League of Gentlemen

—Genuine Jamaican ginger cake? What do you mean, *genuine*? They've never been anywhere near Jamaica!
—What's that got to do with it? We sell Mars bars, don't we?

Granville and Arkwright, Open All Hours

Well done! And you certainly have been.

Arkwright, Open All Hours

Christmas

Murder in 'Coronation Street'. Paedophilia in 'EastEnders'. It must be Christmas.

Nancy Banks-Smith

Condiments of the Seasoning to you!

Count Arthur Strong, aka Steve Delaney

Come in and have a schooner of Algerian sherry and a gypsy cream.

Cissie Braithwaite, aka Roy Barraclough

Sit yerself down in that chair, yonder. That's where my late husband dropped stone dead last Christmas Day. Typical of him, spoiling our Christmas day like that. He was sat there, right as rain, peeling a satsuma, and he suddenly gives this funny little burp and drops forward, dead as a doornail. Typical! Couldn't even wait for the Queen's speech. And as I said to our Pat, what a waste of a satsuma – well, I mean, with the price of citrus fruits these days, every penny counts, doesn't it?

Mrs Partington, *I Didn't Know You Cared*

—Denise, what're we 'avin' for starters tomorrow?
—Well, I'm thinking of Cup-a-Soup – but with a twist.
—Ooh, what's the twist?
—It's going to be in a bowl not a cup.

Barbara Royle and Denise Best, *The Royle Family*

Why not invite an old person into your home this Christmas time. Spoil them with turkey and all the trimmings, and I think £14.50 is about right to charge them.

Mrs Merton, aka Caroline Aherne

Every year on Christmas Day I like to tell my mother that I'm a lesbian, even though I'm not. It just gets everything going.

Jenny Eclair

The first rule of family Christmases is that nobody is allowed to be upstairs having a good time when they could be in the living room getting on somebody's nerves.

Victoria Wood

—What was Christmas like in the old days?
—Same as it is now. Diabolical to the spirit and remorseless to the bowels.

Carter Brandon and Uncle Mort, *Charades With Uncle Mort*

I'm off to do a Yuletide log!

Jim Royle, *The Royle Family*

We couldn't afford a turkey at Christmas. Bert used to give the budgie chest-expanders. The following year, things got better, we had a Peruvian woodcock – black pudding with a feather stuck in it. It was five-a-side to a cracker.

Ada Shufflebottom, aka Les Dawson

—These peas are a bit big.
—They're sprouts.

Morecambe and Wise

—What're we 'avin' for pudding, Denise?
—Well, I'm just gonna go down the traditional Christmas route.
—Ooh, Walls Viennetta!

Barbara Royle and Denise Best, *The Royle Family*

The box of Mon Cheri was pronounced Moan Shereeee, and distributed to Dad and me in single units only, on Christmas Day.

Jeanette Winterson

And then what do the women do? Give you presents you don't want and stare at you till you smile.

Uncle Mort, *I Didn't Know You Cared*

—I got you socks. They're 'every day socks' with the day of the week wrote on them – Monday, Tuesday, Wednesday...
—All right, I get the idea, I'm not bloody Forrest Gump, you know... I

wish you'd got me some 'every day' undies, it's been Sunday all week in these buggers!

Barbara and Jim Royle, The Royle Family

You know the song, 'I Saw Mommy Kissing Santa Claus', I come downstairs, and she's straddling him, she's riding him for all he's worth! I just stood there. I wouldn't eye him, I knew it was me dad dressed up and I thought, thank you, God, cos for the first time in my life me mum and dad weren't arguing – they were making love! And on that Christmas morning, I stood there and watched them for a good twenty minutes. And then me dad come through the door, dressed up as Metal Mickey.

Johnny Vegas

Nobody got bicycles and PlayStations in the Bible, did they, and I'll tell you why: they couldn't afford them. The people in the Bible would have considered themselves very lucky if Father Christmas had brought them a tangerine and Cluedo never mind a bicycle.

Count Arthur Strong, aka Steve Delaney

I bought Mary a pressure cooker. Also, some of those anti-static pads that you put at the end of a sweeper to clean up the dust. I know what Mary's got for me: a pair of ear-defenders and a high-visibility jacket so that I can cut the hedge at dusk and be safe.

John Shuttleworth, aka Graham Fellows

—Are you buying Terry a present this year?
—Yes.
—He never gets you one.
—Yes he does. He got me a goldfish in 1962. It was in a bowl and everything. If he'd put some water in, it might have been alive.

Thelma and Bob Ferris, Whatever Happened to the Likely Lads?

All a bloke really wants for Christmas is a voucher that says: 'Take this to 32, Sycamore Avenue. Mrs Sharratt Farsbarns will be stark naked, waiting for you. You can have as long as you like. You get a cup of tea afterwards, and you don't have to have a bloody conversation.'

Tony, *Dinnerladies*

If there's anything worse than spending Christmas with your own family, it's spending Christmas with somebody else's family, because then not only will you be bored, miserable, irritable and bloated, as you would be in your own home, you will also be completely baffled: 'Oh, yes, we always sing "Little Donkey" in 8-part harmony in the garden at midnight.'

Victoria Wood

News from Westminster is that there is to be no Nativity tableau this year. It's not for religious reasons, just that they can't find three wise men and a virgin. There is no problem, however, in finding enough asses to fill the stable.

Jeremy Paxman

I shall be completely Wenceslassed.

Ken Dodd

Foreign Travel

Every time I go on holiday, the wife gets pregnant. So I'm taking her with me next year.

Roy 'Chubby' Brown

[*Andy and Flo are at the travel agent's*] Basically, we're looking for a place where he can do exactly the same as he does at home but with shorts on.

Flo Capp

Though I had spent some time as a boy with my mother's relatives in Gloucestershire, like most Yorkshiremen I thought that Africa began at Sheffield.

Denis Healey

I was demoralized when I left Bradford for Florida...

Frederick Delius

I like going abroad, but I can't go anywhere for longer than a week, because I start missing my sofa.

Leigh Francis

Four suitcases for Posh Spice? In the 1950s I knew an elderly farmer who embarked on the only holiday of his long lifetime – a trip to the Isle of Man. He stood, in best suit and polished boots, waiting for my father to drive him to the railway station. 'Where is your suitcase?' asked my father. The old man produced a spare shirt collar from his pocket. 'Nay, lad,' he said. 'I'm only going for the week.'

John Mellin

We went on holiday to a little Greek island. We got there and the wife started moaning straight away. 'I love the long mirror, but the room's tiny.' I said, 'We're in the lift.'

Roy 'Chubby' Brown

—Does she like Spain?
—She likes the majesty and grandeur of the landscape, but she's not keen on the bacon.

Faith and Philippa, *Victoria Wood, As Seen on TV*

—What did you eat when you were in Spain?
—I had paella.
—What sort of pie is that?

Mrs Ferris and Bob Ferris, *The Likely Lads*

—You hardly know you've been abroad.
—I know, all right, mate. She'd never have done in Barrow-in-Furness what she did in Tossa del Mare.

Bob Ferris and Terry Collier, *The Likely Lads*

You could tell 'em a mile off, English girls abroad, with their peeling shoulders and flowery dresses – like wallpaper on the march.

Bob Ferris, *The Likely Lads*

The fake tan is a marvellous invention... While everyone else is on the beach trying to go brown, you're in the hotel shagging a waiter.

Jenny Eclair

Look, it's a postcard from Ruby and Chalkie in Paris – Ruby says the Eiffel Tower, the Seine and the Arc de Triomphe are magnificent. Chalkie says the beer tastes funny.

Flo Capp

The problem with France is that, like Wales, it is a very pretty country spoiled only by the people who live there.

Jeremy Clarkson

In Belgium, I attempted a personal challenge to eat my own bodyweight in Belgian chocolate. After the first couple of kilos in the art gallery, the Magritte picture appeared to be moving. After a few more, in a chocolate haze, I heard the voice of Tintin telling me to kill the Smurfs.

Ross Noble

Did you know that over a hundred roadsweepers a year are drowned in Venice?

Ken Dodd

—That's the highest spire in Europe.
—So what? In my day, I had the loudest fart in Europe. But I didn't make a meal out of it.

Carter Brandon and Uncle Mort, *Uncle Mort's South Country*

I used to like America very much. Until I went there.

Jeremy Clarkson

Los Angeles is a very pleasant place as long as you don't meet people.

Morrissey

—What's your love-life like in Los Angeles?
—The sex is nothing to write home about. It's a shame because my mum loves those letters.

Reporter and Robbie Williams

I once asked a friend what India was really like. He thought for a bit and then answered: 'It is like Ashton-Under-Lyne, only hotter.'

James Agate

—How was Cuba?
—Oh, you know. Cuban.

Tom and Sadie King, *Emmerdale*

I was in a Dunkin' Donuts in Canada, and the menu was in French – the whole thing. And I asked the woman for a coffee, and she only spoke French. Now, I've taken a lot of drugs in my time, but I've got to say that the single most frightening experience of my life was thinking, 'I could have swore I was in fuckin' Canada when I got off that tour bus. And now I'm in... am I? No, I don't know...' And then I said to the woman, 'You can speak English, can't you?' And I think she was getting annoyed that I was being a bit rude by that point, because she was only speaking French. I was going, 'I know you can speak English. We're in Canada. And I know you understand what I'm saying.' I may have brought up something about the war and then left.

Noel Gallagher

—What's Monte Carlo like?
—About the same size as Accrington.

Michael Parkinson and Russell Harty

I'm only 5 foot 6 inches, but you feel like Gulliver when you go to Mexico.

Ricky Hatton

I really like Mexican people. I find them terribly nice. And they have fantastic hair.

Morrissey

124

—What is your all-time best travel tip?
—If you end up in a Turkish prison, don't sign up for the ballroom dancing classes.

Interviewer and Ross Noble

I always wanted to go to Nairobi... Just so I could say, 'It's a jungle out there.'

John Cooper Clarke

You can't go abroad with little children. It's not worth spending all that money to fly to some exotic location to spend two weeks in the bedroom with the curtains shut, singing, 'The wheels on the bus go round and round.'

Victoria Wood

—All travel does is breed a nation of malcontents... Why go all the way to Spain to be miserable when you can be miserable on your own front doorstop at Bridlington?
—Mm. And Morecambe, too.
—No, not Morecambe. Moderation in all things, Carter.

Uncle Mort and Carter Brandon, *Uncle Mort's North Country*

Oh I Do Like To Be Beside The Seaside: Northern Seaside Holiday

The lovely vulgar mistress that is Blackpool, always beckoning with a saucy finger to the thrills she can offer.

Les Dawson

Rhyl – for people who think Blackpool's a bit too la-di-da.

Jeff Green

—We used to come on holiday here year after year after year.
—Oh aye? And did you enjoy it?
—Good God, no. You don't go on a holiday to the seaside in the North to enjoy yourself. You go there as an annual penance.

Uncle Mort and Carter Brandon, *Uncle Mort's North Country*

I thought I'd go to one of those little bed and breakfast hotels on the prom... There's nothing in the room, just a single bed and a pedal bin with a notice on it saying: 'This is Not a Bidet.'

Victoria Wood

The landlady said, 'Have you got a good memory for faces?' I said, 'I have.' She said, 'You'll need one cos there's no mirror in the bathroom.'

Ken Goodwin

I went upstairs and washed my hands. I said to the landlady, 'Where's the towel?' She said, 'There isn't one. You'll have to hang your hands out the window.' I'm glad I didn't have a bath.

Ken Goodwin

The misery of holidays! Two weeks of wishing you weren't so fat and shouting at the kids. If you go self-catering, you end up doing exactly the same as you do at home but with different pots and pans.

Jenny Eclair

People who go to caravan sites... I just don't understand these people who can only have a relaxed vacation if they're accompanied at all times by their own washing-up brush.

Victoria Wood

We will be so happy in this, our Tardis on wheels. Our Love Tardis!

Mary Taylor, to Norris Cole, in a motor home, *Coronation Street*

The only time I'm free is when I'm driving the car that tows the caravan on holiday. For those two weeks I wear the trousers. When we get back, I have to have a little cry.

Leo Beckett, husband of Margaret Beckett, MP

A traditional day is to take a trip to the coast to watch the waves lash the rocks and the spray join the driving rain. 'It makes a change even if you don't enjoy it,' as one tripper said.

Joe Ging

It's nobbut watter.

George Metcalfe, Yorkshireman who had never seen the sea

The late Mrs Winterson had a bathing costume made from black-out material... Known in the trade as Suicide Suits, these costumes were so heavy that anything other than paddling in the shallows meant death by sinkage. This didn't worry my mother; Jesus was her lifebelt.

Jeanette Winterson

When it rained, which it did for a large chunk of our holiday, we spent it in bus shelters and shop doorways. Umbrellas were an unnecessary expense, affordable only by bank managers, local officials and the well-off.

Eric Sykes, *If I Don't Write It, Nobody Else Will*

It may be sticky but I never complain. It's nice to have a nibble at it now and again.

George Formby, on his little stick of Blackpool rock

It's all right going on your holidays, but when you get back home, your dishcloth's as stiff as buckram.

M. Bradshaw, overheard

The Natural World

Turned Out Nice Again: Weather

—Super day!
—If you like that sort of thing.

Young Woman and Uncle Mort, *Uncle Mort's South Country*

By Jove, missus! What a beautiful day for putting your kilt on upside down and saying, 'How's that for a shuttlecock?'

Ken Dodd

It was so sunny today I thought I'd been deported.

Charlie Williams

I can't stand the sun. It's such a bloody show-off. The bloody thing comes swaggering into the sky like a Liverpool bucko with a shiny arse to his trouser seat and it screams out, 'Hey up, look at me... Stop what you're doing and come outside and look at me. Bloody thing. Give me a good thin drizzle any day of the week. A drizzle knows its place in life. It just gets on quietly with its job of making everyone thoroughly miserable.

Uncle Mort, *Uncle Mort's North Country*

It were always raining in Denley Moor...'cept on days when it was fine.

Eric Olthwaite, *Ripping Yarns: The Testing of Eric Olthwaite*

People think it always rains in Manchester; not true, although I admit it's the only town in the country with lifeboat drill on the bus routes.

Les Dawson

Me dad always says the weather in Manchester's like the Muslims in Iraq – it's either sunni or it's shiite.

Jason Manford

[*to the pianist*] Right, Mr Braithwaite, 'The Sun Will Come Out Tomorrow'. [*to herself*] Fat chance.

Mrs Wilkinson, *Billy Elliot*

On entering the grandstand... I stood next to an elegantly dressed southern woman who was saying to her male companion, 'It doesn't seem to have dried up much, does it?' To appreciate the full poignancy of the remark, I should mention that she looked as though she had just fallen into the river Ouse.

Andrew Martin, on York's hosting of Royal Ascot, 2005

The weather will be brighter in the north than the south – like the people.

Brian Redhead

My father to this day greets a freezing morning with the observation that 'it's cold enough for two hairnets', while a particularly dark night is 'black as inside of a cow'.

Wendy Holden

The first fall of snow is not only an event but it is a magical event. You go to bed in one kind of world and wake up to find yourself in another quite different, and if this is not enchantment, then where is it to be found?

J.B. Priestley

—It's really icy out there. I slipped coming out of the supermarket and dropped all the shopping.
—Careful opening my beer, then – it'll be a bit lively.

Flo and Andy Capp

It was so cold that the local flashers were handing out written descriptions.

Roy 'Chubby' Brown

—Isn't t'weather terrible?
—Aye, but it's better than nowt.

Joan Bradshaw, overheard in Yorkshire

There's no such thing as bad weather, only unsuitable clothing.

Alfred Wainwright

I was out walking with my relatives in my native Peak District and I was wearing a Harris tweed suit with walking breeches and a fitted jacket. Everyone else was wearing these modern anoraks and I was the only one who stayed dry.

Vivienne Westwood

A blizzard-hit sojourn in the Rookhope Inn passed more easily thanks to a copy of 'Tales From a Long Room'... though locals barely gave the snow a thought. Bobby Bright, a retired rat catcher, had been collecting his morning papers at the post office. 'There's nowt matter wi' t'weather,' he said. 'It's January, a perfect time for winter.'

Mike Amos, *The Northern Echo*

I didn't know what 'wuthering' was until we moved to Yorkshire: the wind is positively vocal and fierce enough to whip you off your feet. The day we moved in, a friendly farmer pronounced, 'By, you get some weather here, but you live forever!'

Sally Kingsley (F)

I used to say: 'In winter I exist, in summer I live.'

Hannah Hauxwell, Daleswoman

—It's your classic stop indoors weather, is this. It's a day to stoke the fire, raid the biscuit tin and annoy your mother. Only a raving idiot would think of setting foot over the front door step.
—Mm. 'Course we could always go down to the pub.
—Right. Now you're talking sense, lad.

Uncle Mort and Carter Brandon, *Uncle Mort's North Country*

Countryside

The North has a hard beauty. It is not a country for the feeblehearted.

Roy Hattersley

It's important to be able to tell the difference between a ripe bilberry and a fresh sheep dropping.

Alfred Wainwright

Pat Wall, chairman of Bradford Trades Council...said he thought people in Bradford weren't too badly off because they had the moors. A man didn't feel puny or oppressed with land all round him.

Beryl Bainbridge, *English Journey*

[*gazing at a spectacular view of the dales*] Everytime I come up here, the spirit soars! You can't help thinking what a wonderful place it would be to set up a machine gun! Give me a small squad of hand-picked men and I could defend this place indefinitely!

Walter 'Foggy' Dewhurst, *Last of the Summer Wine*

I have decided that the best thing to do with the view is to eat it.

Jeremy Clarkson, on taking up shooting

it's great having the Lake District on your doorstep until you have to donkeystone it

Hovis Presley, title of poem

Alfred Wainwright himself went on his final trip to Haystacks in 1991, his ashes carried up by his wife, Betty, to become a bit of grit in a walker's boot.

Eric Robson, *Outside Broadcaster*

Environment

Global warming has just replaced God. Something to feel guilty about. The new religion.

David Hockney

There is no doubt that the world is warming up, but let's just stop and think for a moment what the consequences might be. Switzerland loses its skiing resorts? The beach in Miami is washed away? North Carolina gets knocked over by a hurricane? Anything bothering you yet? It isn't even worth a shrug.

Jeremy Clarkson

My belief is that the green craze, at its maddest – which is what we are going through just now – will pass over like the Hula-Hoop.

Keith Waterhouse, 2008

We've always had pollution. The North East invented pollution long before it became fashionable down south.

Terry Collier, *Whatever Happened to the Likely Lads?*

Bloody Southerners. They don't even know how to despoil the countryside proper, do they? Look at all the hard work we've put in buggering up the North...pit heaps, scummy rivers blighted with chemicals, slimy canals, mill chimneys belching sulphur, cooling towers, sewerage outfalls, dead-eyed estuaries, catarrh, bronchitis, shrivelled lungs, hollow coughs, unimportant deaths. Bloody hell, we're the greatest exporters of acid rain in the whole world. Not like these effete, self-satisfied bastards in the South. The only contribution they've made to the despoliation of Mother Nature is golf courses.

Uncle Mort, *Uncle Mort's South Country*

The Green Belt is Labour policy and we intend to build on it.

John Prescott

The earth is nobler than the world we have put upon it.

J.B. Priestley

Animals

I love animals – especially in good gravy.

Freddie Starr

My father bought me what I thought was a homing pigeon. It was a budgie on an elastic band.

Roy 'Chubby' Brown

—What's the difference between a banker and a pigeon?
—A pigeon can leave a deposit on a Lamborghini.

Vince Cable, *Have I Got News For You*

At the end of January residents in the Northstead area of Scarborough were claiming to have heard the first cuckoo. But yesterday, Mr Hezekiah Johnson, a corporation road-cleaner, said, 'I wait until a crowd gathers at the Northstead bus-stop and then I go into the park nearby and do the cuckoo. They all take it in.' He added, 'I used to do the nightingale when I had my teeth in.'

The Times

Love birds? In Burnley, we call 'em budgies.

Eric Knowles

Two cows chewing grass on a warm, sunny hillock;
I thought, this time tomorrow that grass will be millock.

Eric Morecambe

—Has anyone seen me ferret?
—Yeah, looks like a stretched-out rat.

Daz Eden and Donna Windsor, *Emmerdale*

An upturned hairbrush makes an ideal emergency bed of nails for a hamster.

Top tip, *Viz* magazine

That fool of a tortoise is out again.

Alan Bennett, overheard

—Why don't you just buy your mam a new tortoise if she's that upset.
—Well, we would do, but you never get two the same, do you?

Joe and Joan Bell, *Early Doors*

—Can you hire a camel?
—Yes, there's a little screw underneath the saddle.

Robert Morley (F) and Eric Morecambe, *The Morecambe and Wise Show*

She's got a farm – four chickens and pig. The pig goes round on three legs and one crutch. I said, 'What's the idea of the crutch?' She said, 'We wanted a leg of pork, but we didn't have the heart to kill it.'

'The Little Waster', aka Bobby Thompson

Giraffes have got really long necks and they only eat certain leaves at the top of trees, which is stroke of luck, isn't it?

Boothby Graffoe

A fella's stood at the bus stop, eating a meat pie, in his wellies. There's a woman there, with a poodle. The poodle's jumping up for a bit of the meat pie. He said, 'Missus, can I throw your dog a bit?' She said, 'Yes!' So he threw the dog a hundred yards up the road.

George Roper

I can't abide dogs – great doleful faces, running noses, dropping hairs all over the sofa – they remind me too much of my late husband.

Mrs Partington, *I Didn't Know You Cared*

Dog owners: give passers-by the impression that your dog is well trained by ordering it to do whatever it happens to be doing already.

Top tip, *Viz* magazine

Our cat? Oh, it's finished. It smells, you know, too. It wants doin' away with. Yes, it'll 'ave to go. I could smell it in t'custard on Sunday.

Norman Evans, *Over the Garden Wall*

A Lancashire lad goes to the vet's, flat cap, white raincoat, Woodbine. He says, 'I've come about me cat. It's poorly.' The vet says, 'Is it a tom?' He says, 'No, I brought it with me.'

Bernard Manning

Arts and Entertainment

Classical Music

Ladies and gentlemen, where would we be without good music? Here!

Les Dawson

—I didn't know you could play the piano?
—Oh, it's just for my own amusement really.
—Nobody else thinks it's funny.

Ivy, Cyril Blamire and Norman Clegg, *Last of the Summer Wine*

—You're playing all the wrong notes!
—I'm playing all the right notes, but not necessarily in the right order.

André Previn (F) and Eric Morecambe

Andy Preview – charming man but a rotten pianist... He never went near the black notes.

Eric Morecambe

I took up the flute some years ago, but abandoned it because it made the dog howl.

Sir Tom Courtenay

Like sex and glass-blowing, there must be a point at which [playing the violin] stops being a taxing, traumatic ordeal forever poised on the edge of disaster, and starts becoming really fantastic. I never reached that point.

Stuart Maconie, *Cider With Roadies*

The bagpipes sound exactly the same when you have finished learning them as when you start.

Sir Thomas Beecham

It's an odd thing but a thousand bagpipers are no worse – if I may put it like that – than one. The noise does not seem to get any louder, only more edgy and irritable like live tinned bees.

Nancy Banks-Smith, on the opening of the Commonwealth Games in Edinburgh, 1986

I Took my Harp to a Party But Nobody Asked me to Play

Song title, recorded by Gracie Fields

The harpsichord sounds like two skeletons copulating on a corrugated roof.

Sir Thomas Beecham

The saxophone is the embodied spirit of beer.

Arnold Bennett

Brass bands are all very well in their place – outdoors and several miles away.

Sir Thomas Beecham

—You know what I want for my birthday? A balalaika.
—OK. I'll see if I can get one knitted for you.

Granville and Arkwright, *Open All Hours*

It was all very quiet. Didn't see a soul, not even Ben Britten's. There was a fanfare, but it wasn't one of mine. Bliss, I suppose.

William Walton, composer, while gravely ill in hospital

If any of us were to die and then wake hearing the opening of Mozart's Piano Concerto No.23 in A major, we should know at once that (after all) we had got to the right place.

Neville Cardus

Conducting

There are two golden rules for an orchestra: start together and finish together. The public doesn't give a damn what goes on in between.

Sir Thomas Beecham

Edward Elgar is furious with me for drastically cutting his A Flat Symphony – it's a very long work, the musical equivalent of the Towers of St Pancras Station – neo-Gothic you know.

Sir Thomas Beecham

—What have we got this morning?
—The *Pathétique*, Sir Thomas.
—Oh, well, let's see what we can do to cheer it up.

Orchestra Leader and Sir Thomas Beecham

Gentlemen in the bass department, you will observe in this movement a prolonged *obbligato* passage for the contra-bass meandering through the lower reaches of the orchestra like an amiable tapeworm – may we try it?

Sir Thomas Beecham

—Bass trombone, you are out of tune!
—The bass trombonist hasn't arrived yet.
—Oh. Well, when he arrives, tell him he's out of tune.

Sir Thomas Beecham and Orchestra Member

[*to a trombone player*] —You are new, aren't you? What's your name?
—Ball, sir.
—How very singular.

Sir Thomas Beecham and Mr Ball

[*to a trombone player*] Are you producing as much sound as possible from that quaint and antique drainage system which you are applying to your face?

Sir Thomas Beecham

[*after a tuba player hits a bum note*] Thank you, and now would you pull the chain?

Sir Thomas Beecham

[*to a lady cellist*] Madam, you have between your legs an instrument capable of giving pleasure to thousands – and all you can do is scratch it.

Sir Thomas Beecham

Now I'm going to play the Overture to William T'Hell.

Sir Thomas Beecham, imitating Robb Wilton

—Thank you for a delightful evening with Beecham and Mozart.
—Why drag in Mozart?

Fritz Reiner (F) and Sir Thomas Beecham, after Beecham gave a performance of a Mozart opera in New York

Oh, to be a conductor, to weld a hundred men into one singing giant, to build up the most gorgeous arabesques of sound, to wave a hand and make the clamouring strings sink to a mutter, to wave again, and hear the brass crashing out in triumph, to throw up a finger, then another and another, and to know that with every one the orchestra would bound forward into a still more ecstatic surge and sweep, to fling oneself forward, and for a moment or so keep everything still, frozen, in the hollow of one's hand, and then to set them all singing and soaring in one final sweep, with the cymbals clashing at every flicker of one's eyelid, to sound the grand Amen.

J.B. Priestley

—Who conducted this afternoon?
—Sorry, I forgot to look.

James Agate and Alec Whittaker, first oboe, BBC Symphony Orchestra

T'fat Lady Sings: Opera

—Leonard and I are going to the opening of 'La Traviata' tonight.
—You won't catch me eating that foreign muck.

> Cissie Braithwaite and Ada Shufflebottom, aka Roy Barraclough and Les Dawson

At a performance in English of Richard Strauss's opera, 'Salome', at the Leeds Grand Theatre, Salome danced, Herod asked what she demanded, Salome repeatedly asked for John the Baptist's head, and during a momentary pause in the frenzied music a lady was heard whispering to her neighbour: '*What* did she say she wanted?'

> Michael Meadowcroft

One of the drawbacks of opera in English, where everything that is sung or said can be instantly understood, is that our public, which has a lively sense of humour, never misses an opening for a laugh.

> Sir Thomas Beecham

'The Magic Flute' is the only opera in existence that might conceivably have been composed by God.

> Neville Cardus

[*to a soprano rehearsing the dying Mimi in the last act of 'La Bohème'*]
—More tone! I can't hear you!
—Sir Thomas, one cannot give one's best when one is in a horizontal position.
—Madam, I have given some of my best performances in that position.

> Sir Thomas Beecham and Soprano

If I ever forget my lines, I just sing, 'Kiss my arse, I come from Leeds.' It usually fits everything.

Lesley Garrett, opera singer

That soprano's voice reminds me of a cart coming downhill with the brake on.

Sir Thomas Beecham

Disgusting spectacle, but gad, what a critic!

Sir Thomas Beecham, after a live horse left a 'deposit' during a rehearsal of Verdi's *Aida*

Rock On, Tommy: Popular Music

Every year on the anniversary of Elvis's death, we are bombarded with Elvis films on TV and Elvis records on the radio all day. How can we be assured the same thing won't happen when Michael Ball dies?

Mrs Merton, aka Caroline Aherne

—Next on 'Top of the Pops', it's David Cassidy!
—Ooh, I used to have him on my bedroom wall.
—That was very athletic of you, Janice.

John Peel and Janice Long

That was the best song I've heard since – well, tea time. Mind you, I had a late tea.

John Peel, on a Duran Duran song

Well, that was powerfully average.

John Peel, on a Bruce Springsteen track

Captain Beefheart and the Magic Band Trout Mask Replica sounds like you feel when you've taken the wrong drugs, like going to your mate's dope party on speed.

Peter Hook

Well, that's heavy metal guitar playing, or I'm a Dutchman... This is the Jan Van Der Peel show...

John Peel, after playing 'Hear Nothing, See Nothing, Say Nothing' by Discharge

I'm writing Kylie Minogue's biography. It's called: 'Superstar – Jesus Christ!'

Barry Cryer

One would hear more vocal passion from an ape under anaesthetic.

Morrissey, reviewing 'Golden Days' by Bucks Fizz

Joblessness, glamour and charm in the face of sullen circumstances, lovelorn musings, lust, furtive encounters, politics, the landscape of the North – The Smiths took all these things and elevated them into poetry.

Stuart Maconie, *Cider With Roadies*

The Smiths was like launching your own diary to music.

Morrissey

—How do you choose songs for your live sets?
—I usually pick the songs I'm sure people would least like to hear. And I'm never wrong. If I don't give people something to complain about then I've failed.

Fan and Morrissey

The Smiths' 'Meat is Murder' album is Red Wedge music for sexless students. It's like being stuck in a lift with a Manchester University Socialist Workers' Party convention.

Jackie McKeown (F)

—Still writing in the same vein?
—*With* the same vein.

Simon Mayo (F) and Morrissey

Alex Turner's turns of phrase are ambitious – at one point he rhymes 'problem' with 'Rotherham'.

Mark Rice-Oxley (F), on The Arctic Monkeys' frontman

I wrote about what was around me... But some people are so daft they don't understand that writing about Prestwich is just as valid as Dante writing about his inferno.

Mark E. Smith, *Renegade*

You can read Hemingway's 'A Moveable Feast' and come to Paris, sit in a café and drink coffee, and then try and write your novel but it doesn't work... I wrote 'Don't Let Him Waste Your Time' for Nancy Sinatra while running a bath.

Jarvis Cocker

'She Came in Through the Bathroom Window' was written by Paul when we were in New York forming Apple, and he first met Linda. Maybe she's the one who came in the window. She must have. I don't know. Somebody came in the window.

John Lennon

I make songs up in bizarre places. Pushing kids on swings. In the middle of Tesco's.

Richard Hawley

I liked Sandie Shaw's 'There's Always Something There to Remind Me' because it sounded as if she'd just walked in off the street and begun to sing, and strolled back home and bought some chips.

Morrissey

Let me play a song called 'Two Margarines', all about the misery of having two margarines on the go at once. It's a modern problem brought about by the 'two for one' deal at supermarkets – you know, you'll have one margarine on the go, then a second one is inadvertently opened. Now, I always maintain that one should be re-sealed and hidden away until the first one is finished, but Mary, my wife, insists that it's not a problem, let's have two on the go at once, which is *crazy*.

John Shuttleworth, aka Graham Fellows

—Tony, about your theory that there's a music revolution every 13 years...
I disagree with that, I think it's a load of rubbish.
—You're entitled to an opinion. But your opinion is shit.

Reporter and Tony Wilson

—So what's the name of this band you're managing?
—'Exit'. It's a marketing thing. Wherever we play, our name's up in lights.

Denise and Antony Royle, The Royle Family

—Did you enjoy Britpop?
—That's an unanswerable question really. I was drunk for a lot of it.

Michael Odell (F) and Jarvis Cocker, Q magazine

Noel Gallagher is an absolute tosser and he looks like Parker from Thunderbirds.

Elton John (F)

'The Fourth Best Band in Hull'

The Housemartins, self-promotional slogan

Status Quo used to say that the day you're on the front cover of the NME, that's the time you start worrying – I agree with them.

Mark E. Smith, Renegade

Two men were sitting together in a public house, one deaf, the other not. It was the deaf man's turn to buy a round. On reaching the bar, he ordered two pints. 'How much?' asked the deaf man. 'Six pounds,' said the barman, holding up six fingers to confirm the amount. 'That's a lot for two pints,' said the deaf man. The barman pointed out it was to pay for the entertainment. 'What entertainment?' said the deaf man, when he'd finally understood. 'Country and Western,' yelled the barman. Returning to his friend, the deaf man put down the drinks, complaining that they had cost six pounds. 'Why six pounds?' said the other man. 'To pay for the entertainment,' his deaf friend explained. 'What entertainment?' his mate demanded. 'Some cunt from Preston.'

George Melly, Slowing Down

I am the only man who can say he's been in Take That and at least two members of the Spice Girls.

Robbie Williams

The Anarchists's national anthem is an international anthem that consists of 365 raspberries blown in quick succession to the tune of 'Camptown Races'. Nobody has to stand up for it, nobody has to listen to it, and, even better, nobody has to play it.

Mike Harding

—Eminem is the new Morrissey. Discuss.
—'Pigfarmer's Weekly' is the new 'City Life'. Discuss.

Interviewer and Morrissey, *City Life* magazine

The industry is just rife with jealousy and hatred. Everybody in it is a failed bassist.

Morrissey

I've never met a guitarist I like really... They want a say in all the songs but they don't want to fill in the tax forms.

Mark E. Smith, *Renegade*

The Beautiful South have split up due to musical similarities.

Statement issued by The Beautiful South in 2007

I was asked a brilliant hypothetical question by a Belgian journalist. He said: 'If Oasis were to split up, would you ever consider getting back together again?' How do you answer that?

Noel Gallagher

I would rather eat my own testicles than re-form The Smiths, and that's saying something for a vegetarian.

Morrissey

The Fab Four: The Beatles

—What do you think you've contributed to the musical field?
—Records.

Reporter and Ringo Starr

—There are ten thousand people in this auditorium right now. There must be another ten thousand outside. We came in with George Harrison's mother, and there were so many people who recognised her and were banging on her car. Doesn't this bother you after a while?
—Well, it doesn't bother me if they bang on Mrs Harrison's car.

Reporter and Ringo Starr

—You Beatles have conquered five continents. What would you like to do next?
—Conquer six.

Reporter and the Beatles

—How do you rate your music?
—We're good musicians. Just adequate.
—They why are you so popular?
—Maybe people like adequate music.

Interviewer and the Beatles

—What do you believe is the reason you are the most popular singing group today?
—We've no idea. If we did, we'd get four long-haired boys, put them together and become their managers.

Reporter and John Lennon

—I'd like to form a group. The only thing is, I'd have to change my name. I'd have to have a name like Cliff or Rock, something earthy. Let's invite suggestions for an earthy name for me.
—Sod!

Ken Dodd and John Lennon

—The French haven't made up their minds about the Beatles. What do you think of them?
—Oh, we like the Beatles.

Reporter and John Lennon

—What do you do when you're cooped up in a hotel room between shows?
—We ice skate.

Reporter and George Harrison

—How do you feel about teenagers imitating you with Beatles wigs?
—They're not imitating us because we don't wear Beatles wigs.

Reporter and John Lennon

—What do you call that hairstyle you're wearing?
—Arthur.

Reporter and George Harrison

—What's the biggest threat to your careers – the atom bomb or dandruff?
—The atom bomb. We've already got dandruff.

Reporter and Ringo Starr

Somebody said to me, 'But the Beatles were anti-materialistic.' That's a huge myth. John and I literally used to sit down and say, 'Now, let's write a swimming pool.'

Paul McCartney

All this because of John Lennon? Fucking hell, can you imagine the scenes when Ken Dodd goes?

Elderly Man in a Pub, on the outpouring of grief over the death of
John Lennon, noted by Alan Bleasdale

I Bet You Look Good On The Dancefloor: Dance

—Do you ever go out dancing?
—Heavens no! I can only do that in front of four thousand people. It's the answer to everything.

Interviewer and Morrissey

—The point of dancing is to tone you up, to keep yer muscles supple, to make yer skin tingle.
—You can get that from a mustard bath.

Annie Brandon and Uncle Mort, *I Didn't Know You Cared*

I love the startling intimacy which the tango can engender with a total stranger in a few shocking moments.

Maureen Lipman

151

The full repertoire of Northern soul moves...combined the natural exuberance of dancing with the athleticism and show-offiness of a parallel bars routine.

Stuart Maconie, *Cider With Roadies*

—What does it feel like when you're dancing?
—Don't know. Sort of feels good. It's sort of stiff and that... but once I get going... then I, like, forget everything...and...sort of disappear... Like I feel a change in me whole body. Like there's a fire in me body. I'm just there...flying...like a bird. Like electricity. Yeah... like electricity.

Tutor and Billy Elliot, *Billy Elliot*

Who would have thought that big fat Yorkshire pudding would become such a twinkle toes?

Len Goodman (F), judge, on Darren Gough, 'Strictly Come Dancing'

Knowing the public voted for me made me feel right warm – like an 'amster wearing a Parka.

Keith Lemon, aka Leigh Francis, on winning his heat of
'Let's Dance for Comic Relief'

We made the buggers hop, what?

Sir Thomas Beecham, after playing the dances in *Prince Igor* at very brisk
tempo during the Diaghilev ballet season

Fame and Celebrity

—More than anything else, I wanted to become a star. I wrote to the BBC, telling them what I could do.
—And they wrote back, telling you what you could do.

Ernie Wise and Eric Morecambe

In my day, people would resolve to do something, now they resolve to be someone.

Margaret Thatcher

I've nothing against anyone following their dreams – but not if they're crap.

Robbie Williams

You can rely on Yorkshire people to talk straight. An old man in Barnsley said to me, 'So, you're Jack Parkinson's lad. What you been up to?'

Michael Parkinson, 2008

Fame hits you really hard – like a juggernaut. You deal with it two ways: drink and drugs.

Noel Gallagher

—What is the greatest myth about fame?
—That someone somewhere consequently wants to sleep with you.

Interviewer and Morrissey

I often get people who say, 'I know you. Who are you?' I always think that's very rude, so I'll come up with someone else. I might say, 'I'm Frank Bruno.'

Vic Reeves

When I had a heart attack in Leeds, I was helpless in my Jensen at 1am and the only living person around me was this man who'd been in the Territorial Army. He drove my £7,000 motor car like a tank. As they wheeled me into intensive care he bent over me and whispered, 'Can I have your autograph before you go?'

Eric Morecambe

People never ask me for my autograph. They think I look too grumpy to approach. What they don't understand is that I always look like this.

Noel Gallagher

—Hi, I'm Jeremy Clarkson, I do *Top Gear*.
—[*not recognizing him*] Are you trying to sell me drugs?

Jeremy Clarkson and Kate Moss, at a film première

It's a funny thing this celebrity. If you don't wave back you're a miserable bugger; if you do wave back you're a big-headed bugger. I don't know.

Fred Dibnah, steeplejack

—It's like people think us celebs all shop at a Celebrity Asda or something. We're normal people. It's nothing like that.
—It is. It's just you're never invited.

Les Dennis and Sean Lock, *8 Out of 10 Cats*

You know Neil Armstrong, the astronaut fellow, say you met him and got talking to him, 'ow long d'you think you could go before you mentioned the moon? I'm always thinking about that.

Joe, *Early Doors*

I met William Shatner once, in a lift. He got in a lift we were in and we actually did resist the urge as he pushed the button to his floor, to say, you know what I'm gonna say, don't you? I don't need to say it. But we all burst out laughing because we all wanted to say it.

Noel Gallagher

—Can we take a photo of your house?
—Of course you can. You paid for it.

Fan and Noel Gallagher, outside 'Supernova Heights'

People are always sending me pictures of their aspidistras.

Gracie Fields

I was sitting at a Variety Club luncheon with Maggie Smith, and someone came up to the table and asked me for my autograph. I was so bamboozled by the fact that they'd asked me and not her that I signed it Maggie Smith.

Maureen Lipman

Richard Whiteley told me of addressing a vast crowd in Bradford. He shouted at them: 'Can you all hear me?' A man sitting halfway down the hall shouted back: 'I can, but I don't mind changing places with someone who can't!'

W.R. Mitchell, *Yorkshire Post*

The English instinctively admire any man who has no talent and is modest about it.

James Agate

There's nothing the British like better than a bloke who comes from nowhere, makes it, and then gets clobbered.

Melvyn Bragg

The high spot of Tommy Forrest's life was when he met the Pope. A neighbour pointed to a photo of the two of them in the 'Ilkley Gazette' and asked, 'Who's that with Tommy Forrest?'

Alan Titchmarsh, *Nobbut a Lad*

I am possibly the only person in Liverpool of a similar age to John Lennon, had he lived, who claims never to have met him. Or, indeed, any of the Beatles. Believe me, everyone else had met one of the Beatles by 1963... This fame by association reached its zenith when a member of our chess club announced that his Alsatian had impregnated Ringo Starr's mother's bitch.

Alan Bleasdale

—Ringo, why do you get the most fan mail?
—I don't know. Perhaps it's because more people write to me.

Reporter and Ringo Starr

I'm warning you with peace and love. I have too much to do. So no more fan mail. Thank you, thank you. And no objects to be signed. Nothing. Anyway, peace and love, peace and love.

Ringo Starr, video message to fans, 2008

Take away the belt, the money, the Jag and people would still like me. What's the point of being a world champion if you're the biggest tosser under the sun?

Ricky Hatton

People say Calum Best is only famous because of who his dad was. But then you could say the same about Jesus.

Karl Pilkington

Madonna was the first to...make the private a public free-for-all. And now she wants her privacy back.... Imagine looking back on your deathbed and remembering the days you spent reading up on these air-wasters. You can switch on the internet and find out what Beyoncé had for breakfast. You don't actually find out about the lyrics of these people, their ideas, etc. What's it for?

Mark E. Smith, *Renegade*

I haven't heard of Antanddec. Is that one person?

Paris Hilton (F)

You know how to tell the difference between Ant and Dec? Ant's on smack, Dec's on crack.

Jonathan Ross (F)

He's like a bloody bad smell that Noel Edmonds. I wish someone'd put 'im in one of those bloody boxes and bury it.

Jim Royle, *The Royle Family*

My dad was very proud of being a Yorkshireman and he said to me, just before he died: 'You've 'ad a good time doing your talk show, 'aven't you, lad? You've made a bob or two, met all them lovely birds and film stars? Think on. Good as that might be, it's not likely playing for Yorkshire at cricket, is it?' In his view, that's what defined immortality not fame.

Michael Parkinson

Theatre and Acting

I was at university in Manchester. I was doing drama – not a course that's gonna take off in the north west. I was trying to do Shakespeare in the second year: 'Is this a dagger I see before me?' 'Yeah, give me yer trainers!'

Jason Manford

My father once said to me: 'What the hell are you doing being an actor? You'll die of starvation, in the rain, on Crewe Station.'

Clive Swift

It was my mother's ambition, not mine, that I should be an actress... I wasn't all that interested myself. Given the choice I would have preferred to run away to sea or else to have worked in some capacity in a mortuary.

Beryl Bainbridge

I'd like to have been a really successful actress but I couldn't do it because I was too vain. As an actress people wouldn't have seen me as being intelligent.

Anne Robinson

Eighty per cent of actors are unemployed. You know why an actor never looks out of the window in the morning? He's got to have something to do in the afternoon.

Maureen Lipman

The most important thing in acting is to be able to laugh and cry. When I have to cry, I think of my love life. When I have to laugh, I think of my love life.

Glenda Jackson

This was an actress who, for twenty years, had the world at her feet. She kicked it away, and the ball rolled out of her reach.

James Agate, on Mrs Patrick Campbell (F)

—Robert Donat is a half-Greek god who has winged his way from Olympus.
—Actually, I'm a half-Pole who's winged his way from Withington, Manchester.

Critic and Robert Donat

In England nobody goes to the theatre unless he or she has bronchitis.

James Agate

The Lord Mayor of Leeds once told me a tale at a literary lunch. It concerned a local production of 'Romeo and Juliet', in which Miss Capulet was played by a somewhat superannuated and extremely buxom lady. On the way out of the theatre post-performance, an admirer was heard to remark: 'That Gladys Arkwright may be no Sarah Bernhardt but, by 'eck, she knows 'ow to lean over a balcony.'

Wendy Holden

159

Babs Osborne... whose features were a little too Frinton-on-Sea to suggest the perfect Cleopatra.

Beryl Bainbridge, *An Awfully Big Adventure*

You couldn't get out of the theatre-in-the-round without crossing the stage. If anyone was ill, it was a nightmare. One night a woman was obviously going to be sick. She couldn't get out, so she opened her handbag. It was distracting.

Malcolm Hebden, actor

Film and Television

There was life before 'Coronation Street', but it didn't add up to much.

Russell Harty

Mondays and Wednesdays I live for them. Thank God, half past seven tonight and I shall be in Paradise.

John Betjeman (F), President of the British League For Hilda Odgen - and poet

I well remember the trauma, as a small child about forty years ago, of accidentally watching an episode of 'Coronation Street', and being told that what I saw was not a documentary-style reconstruction of life in the late Middle Ages.

Simon Heffer (F)

I keep being told 'Coronation Street' has done nothing to enhance the region's reputation. But if it came to a choice between living with the crazy geriatrics and backward teenagers of Weatherfield or the pathological criminals of Walford – where 'EastEnders' live – give me 'Coronation Street'.

Roy Hattersley

If 'EastEnders' is so true to life, how come none of the loveable Cockney characters are Man Utd supporters?

P. Sullivan, *Viz* magazine

Mr Popadopalos owns the launderette in 'EastEnders'. Mr Popadopalos is one of life's great invisibles, like God and Mrs Glum.

Nancy Banks-Smith

Cain Dingle: Liam Gallagher on a tractor.

Grace Dent, on *Emmerdale*

I have this theory that if you watch more than two-and-a-bit soaps you go mad, so my devotion to 'Emmerdale' is intermittent.

Nancy Banks-Smith

If it wasn't for 'Emmerdale' I wouldn't get any fresh air at all.

John Cooper Clarke

Nowt but propaganda is 'Postman Pat'. Early in the morning? When the day is dawning? Your *real* Postman Pat rolls up about noon wearing a pair of shorts and his breakfast. And, if he's not chucking elastic bands like confetti, he'll be rifling through your birthday cards for ready cash, or leaving yer valuables out on the step. And as for Mrs Goggins – she'll be cowering behind three-inch thick glass with a baseball bat under the counter – assuming that her post office hasn't been shut down of course.

Blanche Hunt, *Coronation Street*

Nick Park – Preston's Answer to Walt Disney

Headline, *Sunday Telegraph*

'What's Eating Gilbert Grape?' – imagine sitting through that film twice. I'd rather be on a long-haul flight, in economy class, sat between Terry Christian on one side, and another Terry Christian on the other.

Paul Calf, aka Steve Coogan

—This is my seat of learning, this chair. When I learn from that box, I am at the University of Life... I know the metamorphosis of the frog: it starts out with just dots in the water, 'amoebas' they're called... then you get your frogspawn, then you get this small, black thing, which develops two front legs and a head, then some back legs, and this ends up as a tadpole, and your tadpole becomes a frog...
—And then?
—Well, then it turns into a butterfly.

Terry Collier and Bob Ferris, *Whatever Happened to the Likely Lads?*

Hang The DJ: Radio

Radio is a marvellous invention as it makes you feel like you're the only person that the DJ is talking to. Never is this more true than in the case of Signal Cheshire.

Mrs Merton, aka Caroline Aherne

Disc jockeys: they are the hollow men. They are electronic lice.

Anthony Burgess

The Radcliffe-Maconie partnership already feels like an institution...
Their easy banter is so un-self-conscious, so pass-the-butter-mother
comfortable, they sound like a married couple, albeit a married couple
that doesn't touch one another's bottom, obviously, and spends its
evenings discussing the thematic intricacies of Van der Graaf Generator
records as opposed to, say, skirting boards.

> Sarah Dempster (F), on the Mark Radcliffe and Stuart Maconie Show,
> BBC Radio 2

—Quiet, quiet! It's almost time for the news. [*turns on the radio*]
—This is the BBC radio news at—[*abruptly turns off the radio*]
—That's better. You've no idea what benefit I derive from that regular,
daily, not-listening-to-the-news. It's a public duty these days to keep
yourself ill-informed, I say. Restores a bit of English sanity to English
streets.

> Arkwright and Radio Announcer, *Open All Hours*

How Tickled I Am: Comedy and Clubs

—P.G. Wodehouse defined humour as 'The kindly contemplation of the
incongruous'. What do you think of that?
—He should try the Golden Garter Club in Wythenshawe on a Saturday
night.

> Eric Midwinter and Ken Dodd

I was in Bolton last night. Anyone dies in Bolton, they don't bury them.
They bring them to the club, sit them in the audience and put the comic
on.

> Jackie Hamilton

A young comic is on stage, dying on his feet, when all of a sudden there's a huge roar of approval from the crowd. He looks across at the chairman in the wings, who says, 'Don't worry, it's just the hot pies have come.'

Old clubland joke

It was one of those clubs, when you went to the toilet, on the door of the gents was a penis, so you knew it was the gents. On the ladies was a photograph of the committee.

Jackie Hamilton

With regard to £300 missing from club funds – we will have a word with the treasurer as soon as he gets back from Tenerife.

Colin Crompton

My club is world famous – we get coaches from as far away as Sheffield.

Bernard Manning, on the Embassy Club, Manchester

—[*to the audience*] Are you enjoying yourselves?
—Yes!
—[*frostily*] Why, what are you doing?

Ken Dodd and Audience

'What d'you think of t'comedian?' 'Well, he's all right, if you like laughing.'

Dave Spikey

I can tell a joke in Blackburn and get a huge laugh, yet it won't raise a titter in Blackpool – they can't hear it!

Ken Dodd

I got into stand-up comedy because I thought it'd be sex, drugs and rock 'n' roll. It's ended up being wanking, cough mixture and Billy Ray Cyrus.

Lee Mack

I found myself booked on 'The Billy Cotton Band Show' at the Manchester Opera House with a comedy duo who were so unfunny that when they once did get a laugh it threw their timing and they left the business.

Les Dawson

I'm funny only because I'm experienced at being funny. I practised for ages in front of a mirror putting my glasses on sideways.

Eric Morecambe

In Golcar, they booked me for an Australian themed night. There were Australian flags, a didgeridoo, boomerangs, and everyone had corks on hats. The compère gets on stage, picks up a boomerang and says, 'If I throw this, d'you think it'll come back?' And this bloke at the back shouted, 'If it hits me it fucking will!'

Dave Spikey

—I want my money back.
—I want to moonwalk, son, but life's a shithouse.

Student and [wheelchair-bound] Brian Potter, *Phoenix Nights*

I did the Royal Variety Show and they put me in the same dressing-room with Frank Carson, Stan Boardman, Bernard Manning and Angela Rippon. God, she knows some filthy jokes.

Victoria Wood

Oh, that reminds me, I must buy a stamp.

Jimmy Tarbuck, at the Royal Variety Performance

You're the chicken fella, aren't you? [*handing him a serviette in a fish and chip café*] Put your bloody moniker on here. It's for the wife. She thinks a lot about you, by the hell, she laughs at you. Mind you, she laughs at anything.

'Fan', to Norman Collier, chicken impersonator and virtuoso of the faulty microphone routine

I had to laugh at something my son said the other day. Mind you, he's Chubby Brown.

Ida Brown, *Viz* magazine

My dad said, 'Laughter is the best medicine,' which is why, when I was six, I nearly died of diphtheria: 'Dad, I can't breathe!' 'Knock, knock...'

Dave Spikey

—Knock, knock...
—I'm not in. I refuse to open the door.

Jools Holland (F) and Morrissey, *Later With Jools Holland*

Smiling can be quite a shock to the system if you're not used to it.

Les Brandon, *I Didn't Know You Cared*

Politics and Society

I Predict a Riot: Violence

I'm from Manchester. We got bombed ten years ago by the IRA and I went over to Belfast recently to did a gig. I went out on stage and said, 'Hello, I'm from Manchester,' and a bloke from the back went, [*assumes Northern Irish accent*] 'Did you enjoy the bomb?' Me arse went a bit. I said, 'Er, yeah, we did, actually, thanks. At the end of the day, nobody died, we got a new "Next".'

Jason Manford and Irish Audience Member

He said, 'Want to fight?' I said, 'Who?' He said, 'You.' I said, 'Me?' He said, 'Yes.' I said, 'No.'

Robb Wilton

He said, 'I'll punch yer head.' I said, 'Whose?' He said, 'Yours.' I said, 'Mine?' He said, 'Yes.' I said, 'Oh.'

Robb Wilton

Why is it I want to turn her upside down and pile-drive her into the cobbles?

Eileen Grimshaw, *Coronation Street*

You big girl's blouse!

Nelly Pledge, *Nearest and Dearest*

Oh, you great big mard nelly! I'll take yer with me left hand if she starts anything!

Ena Sharples, to Dennis Tanner, *Coronation Street*

I'd break her bastard teeth if I knew what drawer they were in.

Roy 'Chubby' Brown

It was so hard on the daffodils.

Margaret Thatcher, after being hit on the head by a protestor with a bunch of them during the 1992 election campaign in Stockport

In my day [such negotiations] would have required the occasional use of the handbag. Now it will be a cricket bat. But that's a good thing because it will be harder.

Margaret Thatcher, on John Major's negotiations on the Maastricht Treaty, 1993

I have never been attracted to any kind of violence. I even refused to join the Girl Guides because they wore uniforms.

Kate Adie, war reporter

I think I have a working-class girl's respect for property. In the past, I would never have minded thumping somebody, but I wouldn't have broken their stuff.

Jeanette Winterson

After I punched Piers Morgan, every woman said, 'Why did you hit him?' and every man said, 'Where did you hit him?'

Jeremy Clarkson

Well, I had been told that we had to connect with the electorate directly.

John Prescott, on why he threw a punch at a man during a campaign rally in 2001

The right to bear arms is slightly less ludicrous than the right to arm bears.

Chris Addison

We all agree that firearms are terrible. In fact, I wrote a song called 'Shoot the Gun'.

John Shuttleworth, aka Graham Fellows

—My grandfather gave me this gun when I was a kid. He shot a German with it.
—Was that in the Second World War?
—No, it were in Benidorm. He had a row over a sun lounger.

Max Bygraves and Paddy O'Shea, *Phoenix Nights*

Crime and Punishment

I was living the life of Riley last week – and then the police took his fucking credit cards back off us.

Roy 'Chubby' Brown

Drug addicts have been breaking into churches and stealing everything that wasn't nailed down. So Jesus was all right.

Pauline Calf, aka Steve Coogan

Word from the wise: get yer stuff out quick sharp, otherwise he'll have your stereo in his veins before you can say 'Dolby surround sound'.

Frank Gallagher, *Shameless*

I've always thought, the best thing to do if you hear a burglar, is get stark naked, working on the assumption that no burglar will think there's any possession worth nicking that you've got to wrestle a naked man for.

Jeff Green

Every single scally in Manchester was in Knebworth to see Oasis and where I live, we got a load of middle-class people together, and went and robbed Moss Side.

Chris Addison

No matter what trouble you're going to get into, never get arrested in a country that doesn't use your own alphabet... If you get arrested in a country that uses squiggles instead of proper letters, you're fucked, mate, you're never coming home.

Noel Gallagher

We're lucky in Manchester because the kids have such shit weaponry.

Tony Wilson

It's rough everywhere now. I got my Rolex snatched outside the house. It wasn't real – it was only £2.99. I won't tell the insurance that, of course. Thank God for the Co-op Assurance. When a girl's skint, best thing to do is 'ave a break-in.

Lily Savage, aka Paul O'Grady

Life is *so* depressing. I saw on the news some old woman in London got beaten up for 60 pence. If I were going to beat someone up I'd want a lot more than that for my troubles.

Pauline Calf, aka Steve Coogan

They say you should carry a pot of pepper in yer handbag. What bloody good is that? Unless it's one of those wooden jobs you get in an Italian restaurant. Thwack!

Lily Savage, aka Paul O'Grady

I inquired of my local reference library as to where I might locate their section of books on ethics, for a research project I am involved in. Unhesitatingly, the librarian replied, 'I'm afraid they've all been nicked.'

Julian Corlett

I had to admit that it had been 'a fair cop'. I'd been caught pissing up against a wall in a fairly dark alley off the Uxbridge Road... I explained to the law that every night I have to take a round white pill in order to expel the excess water from my system... The pills' demands are instantaneous. You have about ten seconds between the pressing need and its fulfilment... The policeman stood in thought for some time. Then he passed judgement. 'Well, sir, this time we'll overlook it, but next time try not to use the wall of a police station.'

George Melly, *Slowing Down*

What a detective! Once a burglar robbed a safe wearing calfskin gloves. He took the fingerprints and five days later he arrested a cow in Surrey.

Eric Morecambe

You know when they find a body in the river or the lake or something and they don't know who it is, and the police have to identify them by their dental records, well, how do they know who their dentist is?

Joan Bell, *Early Doors*

'Course, I'm a sergeant, you see. When I say, 'sergeant' I'm *practically* a sergeant – it's only a matter of three stripes, and clothes are quite heavy enough in the warm weather without them.

Robb Wilton

We were on desk duty down at the police station. This woman comes in to report a flasher. All flustered she was. She were walking back from the post office, this bloke pulls up beside her and starts asking her directions. He's got a map in his lap. She's telling him the way and next thing, he pulls the map away, he's got his bloody todger out! She shrieks and he speeds off. Anyway, she's telling us all this and we're having to write it down for the report. She's givin' us a good description of him and then I says to her – and you've got to ask this, by the way – 'Was he in a state of arousal?' And she says, 'No, he was in a Ford Escort.'

Police Constable Phil, *Early Doors*

Closed Circuit Television has driven teenagers out of the city centres, so they queue outside remote farmhouses, waiting for their turn to defecate on an heirloom. And where are the police? Well, they know you're only after a crime number for insurance, so they're about 40 miles away, trimming their moustaches to look good on next week's edition of 'Police. Stop. Kill'.

Jeremy Clarkson

—I'll never forget my mother's words to me when I first went to jail.
—What did she say?
—Hello, son.

Morecambe and Wise

These two fellas are in prison. One says to the other, 'How long are you in for?' 'Three days.' He says, 'How did you manage that?' 'They're hanging me on Monday.'

Ken Goodwin

Would-be criminals: Before you commit a crime, get a foretaste of what the world would look like from inside a prison by holding a fork up close to your eye.

Top tip, *Viz* magazine

Law and Lawyers

There is, in Yorkshire, the legendary story of Gilbert Gray QC who was representing a working man from the town before a judge of particular pomposity who, at one point snootily interjected: 'I take it, Mr Gray, that your client is familiar with the maxim: *Quis custodiet ipsos custodes?*' 'Indeed my lord,' responded the QC drily. 'In Barnsley they speak of little else.'

The Independent

Can you put that in layman's terms, bearing in mind that we are in Preston?

Richard Henriques QC, questioning an expert witness in the trial of
Dr Harold Shipman

In 1964, Alan Brien was being threatened with a libel action by Lord Beaverbrook, the newspaper magnate, over something he had written in one of his columns. At a theatre opening night, as he was sharing a drink with fellow critics, one of them relayed the news that Beaverbrook had just died. Brien was jubilant. 'I feel,' he declared, 'as though someone just told me that Agincourt has been called off.'

Times obituary

At Darlington County Court some years ago, I appeared as counsel in a turgid boundary dispute before the late Judge Cohen, who was listening to a less than enthralling closing speech from my opponent. As he sometimes did, the judge closed his eyes. From the back of the court came the comment from a supporter of my opponent's client, 'The old bugger's gone to sleep!' Judge Cohen opened one eye and replied, 'The old bugger hasn't,' and the trial continued to its appointed end.

Geoffrey W. Davey

The new series of 'Kavanagh QC' is so true to life that I fell fast asleep during the last ten minutes of counsel's speech to the jury.

Judge Barrington Black

Politics and Government

Me, politics? I'd make Mussolini look like Marie Osmond.

Paul O'Grady

My desire to get into Parliament was like miners' coal dust, it was under my fingers and I couldn't scrub it out.

Betty Boothroyd

There will be a groundswell of public opinion sooner or later which will carry me into office. And let me tell you, I'll only be there five years and it'll all end in tears – but it will be a proper, proper laugh while it's happening.

Noel Gallagher, on his aspirations to become prime minister

Can you imagine anything so boring as world domination. I mean, what would you do in your spare time?

Morrissey

—What do you miss most about being deputy prime minister?
—Croquet.

Reporter and John Prescott

Parliament is a club to protect us when we want to hide from wives, mistresses and the media rather as real people have allotments.

Austin Mitchell, MP

Sometimes I find myself thinking, rather wistfully, about Lao Tzu's famous dictum: 'Govern a great nation as you would cook a small fish.' All around me I see something very different, let us say – a number of anxious or angry dwarfs trying to grill a whale.

J.B. Priestley

Your business is not to govern the country but it is, if you think fit, to call to account those who do govern it.

William Ewart Gladstone, to the House of Commons, 1869

—The trouble with England is it's being governed by cunts.
—Quite frankly, old man, there're an awful lot of cunts in England, and they deserve representation.

Rex Harrison and an Unidentified MP

Call me Madam!

> Betty Boothroyd, on being asked how she wished to be addressed on becoming
> Speaker of the House of Commons

Any woman who understands the problems of running a home will be near to understanding the problems of running a nation.

> Margaret Thatcher

Women such as Margaret Thatcher or Bessie Braddock would admit that they don't do charm and that they don't trust people who do. 'Charming!' is an expression of disgust to them.

> Edwina Currie

For me, politics is about encouragement and pushing the right people – sometimes off the balcony.

> Paul Heaton

Canvassing for the Tadcaster West ward in a Selby District Council by-election, I struck up a conversation with a local pensioner. She asked me what party I was standing for and when I told her the Conservatives she replied, 'Oh my dear, I know just how you feel. I'm a Jehovah's Witness.'

> Juliet Peck

I was born in Rotherham. Around where I lived, people thought a Conservative was something you spread on your toast.

> William Hague

William Hague? Oh yeah, the guy who came with the runner.

> George W. Bush (F), recalling a visit by Hague, accompanied by Sebastian Coe

William Hague makes rather good speeches. They've got verbs in them.

> Douglas Hurd (F)

Supporting Manchester United will become a criminal offence for anyone born south of Crewe.

> Monster Raving Loony Party, election manifesto

You wake up and hear [Harold] Shipman has topped himself. And you think, is it too early to open a bottle? Then you discover everybody's upset. You have to be very cautious in this job.

> David Blunkett, Home Secretary, 2004

I have been recasting 'The Wind in the Willows' from the Commons. Would you say Boris Johnson or John Prescott as Toad? Ann Widdecombe as the washerwoman? The weasels and stoats present no problem at all. I am, however, having great difficulty with the modest and endearing Mole.

> Nancy Banks-Smith

I wish I had a machine gun on the lot of you – you are all rats. We have a corporation rat catcher but he goes for the wrong sort.

> 'Battling' Bessie Braddock, Labour MP, to Conservatives in Liverpool City Council Chamber

If Roland Rat were appointed to Northern Ireland I would tell people to work with him, but I would still point out that he was a rat.

William Hague, after Peter Mandelson was appointed
Northern Ireland Secretary, 1999

Peter Mandelson shook hands with Mickey Mouse and noticed he was wearing a Harriet Harman watch.

William Hague, on Peter Mandelson's visit to Disneyworld

When Gordon Brown smiles it looks like it hurts.

Barry Cryer

John Prescott looks like a terrifying mixture of Hannibal Lecter and Terry Scott.

Gyles Brandreth (F)

John Prescott is 70 years old. Once upon a time everyone on Labour's front bench looked like him. Ernie Bevin. Bessie Braddock. Particularly Bessie Braddock.

Nancy Banks-Smith

—Winston, you're drunk.
—Bessie, you're ugly. But tomorrow I shall be sober.

Bessie Braddock and Winston Churchill (F)

I am rather allergic to the Blair Babes, Patricia Hewitt, Ruth Kelly, Hazel Blears – they all talk at you as if they are ticking you off for having dirty shoes at school.

Jilly Cooper

Patricia Hewitt's ability is beyond question. But she would not be my choice as a companion for a walking holiday in the Lake District.

Roy Hattersley

Hazel Blears is like a feral Krankie.

Sandi Toksvig (F)

...perky plucky little condescending tone-deaf self-satisfied self-righteous and self-deluded impertinent busy-body...

Howard Jacobson, on Hazel Blears

The life of a mule harnessed to a wheel can have more excitement than that of the government backbencher in Parliament.

Jeremy Paxman

[*offering encouragement before her first speech to a Conservative Party Conference as Party Leader*] —Peace of cake, Margaret!
—Good heavens! Not now!

Ronald Millar (F) and Margaret Thatcher

—Is the Right Honourable Lady aware that Mr Len Murray insists that when he sees her, it is like having a dialogue with the deaf?
—I had no idea that Mr Murray was deaf.

Sydney Bidwell (F) and Margaret Thatcher

I am not quite certain what my Right Honourable Friend said, but we both hold precisely the same view.

Margaret Thatcher

It is private threats which alter prime ministers' minds. Public threats only polish haloes.

Roy Hattersley

There are no personal sympathies in politics.

Margaret Thatcher

I'd rather people wondered why I wasn't prime minister than wondered why I was.

Denis Healey

Paddy Ashdown is the only party leader who's a trained killer. Although, to be fair, Mrs Thatcher was self-taught.

Charles Kennedy (F)

The Prime Minister says that she has given the French President a piece of her mind – this is not a gift I would receive with alacrity.

Denis Healey, on Margaret Thatcher

To quote her own back-benchers, the Great She-elephant, She-Who-Must-Be-Obeyed, the Catherine the Great of Finchley, the Prime Minister...

Denis Healey, on Margaret Thatcher

The Right Honourable Gentleman is afraid of an election is he? He is frightened, frightened, frit!

Margaret Thatcher, to Denis Healey

I think sometimes the prime minister should be intimidating. There's not much point in being a weak, floppy thing in the chair, is there?

Margaret Thatcher

If she would only occasionally come in with a smut on her nose, her hair dishevelled, looking as if she's been wrestling with her soul, as I do.

Barbara Castle, on Margaret Thatcher

Good Conservatives always pay their bills. And on time. Not like the Socialists who run up other people's bills...

Margaret Thatcher

Thank you for dredging up the horrors of my expenses... Money spent on Ginger Crinkles and Branston Pickle shocks me. Neither is made in Grimsby but I am instituting immediate enquires in my household to see who could possibly be responsible for introducing such dangerous substances. I have not so far traced empty containers of either. Whisky and gin are another matter. I drink neither. I will check to see if my wife is an alcoholic and take appropriate action... I'm sorry I can't comment further as I'm off to a seminar on 'Cleaning and Maintaining your Moat'.

Austin Mitchell, MP, letter to the *Telegraph*

How can you tell if a politician is lying? If he straightens his cuffs, he's telling the truth. If he smoothes his hair, he's telling the truth. If he touches his nose, he's telling the truth. But if opens his mouth...

Maureen Lipman

Is it not the case that those found guilty of fraud are the only people left in the Labour Party with genuine convictions?

William Hague

It's no good laying the blame at anybody's feet. It's no good telling the politicians to go to hell because they're building it for us.

Les Dawson

Many journalists have fallen for the conspiracy theory of government. I do assure you that they would produce more accurate work if they adhered to the cock-up theory.

Bernard Ingham, press secretary to Margaret Thatcher

This place is the longest running farce in the West End.

Cyril Smith, M.P. on the House of Commons

The Day War Broke Out: War and Peace

What on earth was Adolf Hitler thinking of?

Mrs Merton, aka Caroline Aherne

The day war broke out, my Missus said to me – she looked at me and she said, 'What good are you..? What are you supposed to do?' I said, 'I'm supposed to stop Hitler's army landing.' She said, 'What! *You*..?' She said, 'Do you know this Hitler? Have you ever met him?' I said, 'Do I – of course I don't!' She said, 'Well how are you going to know which is him if they *do* land?' I said, 'Well, I've got a tongue in my head, haven't I?'

Robb Wilton

—Hitler only had one ball.
—D'you think that's why he was always in such a bad mood?

Denise and Jocelyn Best, The Royle Family

I can always remember my father shouting upstairs to my mother, 'Come on, love, it's an air raid!' She said, 'Just a minute, I'm looking for my teeth!' He said, 'They're dropping bombs not pies!'

Bobby Knoxall

The army medical was very strict. I said to the doctor, 'You can't take me – I wear glasses.' He said, 'That's all right. We'll put you right in the front so you won't miss anything.'

Eric Morecambe

They won't let dwarves in the army. I say flood the army full of dwarves! Put them in the infantry division, send them over first, and they'd always have the element of surprise because people'd think they were further away than they actually were.

Chris Addison

I didn't join the army to dig holes. If I wanted to spend all my spare time digging holes, I'd have joined the Territorial Gas Board.

Private Tony Lloyd, All Quiet on the Preston Front

During the war, Herbert Ogden spent a whole week's wages on a land-girl with a wiggle like that. All he got were a tip on what to do with his broccoli.

Arkwright, Open All Hours

—Did I ever tell you about my service in the First World War? All them brave lads cut down in their prime. All those sturdy Northerners wiped off the face of the earth, doomed to spend eternity poking their toes at the roots of the poppies in Flanders fields... Sam Chedzoy copped his lot at the Somme, you know. And so did Wallace Crump, Tommy Burrows, Victor Snaith, Wilf Chadwick, Ernie Atkins, Norman and Sid Richings and Lionel Slakehouse with his big ears. I wonder what they'd be doing now, if they was still alive?'
—They'd probably be dead.

Uncle Mort and Carter Brandon, *Uncle Mort's North Country*

I suppose the only thing worse than being blown up by a mortar on Sunday morning is having two senior Conservative Party figures visiting you on a Monday morning.

William Hague, accompanied by David Cameron, on a visit to an injured soldier in Basra, who replied, 'It's about on a par, sir.'

They came, they saw, they made a cup of tea.

Jeremy Paxman, after the Royal Marines' peacekeeping mission in Afghanistan ended

—When Hitler marched into Czechoslovakia, if people had said, 'Peace and Love' to him, it wouldn't have done much good.
—No, but what if they had been saying it to him from the moment he was born?

Sir David Frost (F) and John Lennon

We are prepared to fight for peace.

Margaret Thatcher

Business

By Jove, missus! What a lovely day for walking up to a Muslim
businessman and saying, 'Have you made a profit, Mohammed?'

Ken Dodd

Who do you think you are sat sitting there like a big business typhoon?

Nelly Pledge, Nearest and Dearest

There's endless scope for art and creativity in business – the thrill of
stripping underused assets away from the body of some moribund
company to reveal the vital, throbbing profitable form within. The
greatest works of men are not cast in bronze, they're forged in brass!

Bradley Hardacre, Brass

—You taint and corrupt everything you grasp!
—What you're saying is, I've got on. And if it's a crime to 'ave initiative
and enterprise and take pleasure in the exhilarating cut and thrust of the
marketplace where this country sinks or swims, very well, I plead guilty. I
can't stand 'ere talking all day, I've got men to lay off!

Lady Patience and Bradley Hardacre, Brass

—There's trouble at t'mill. T'workers are upset. They say they've too far
to come to t'mill.
—Too far to come? Nay, but they've only three fields to cross.
—Aye, but they're Huddersfield, Macclesfield and Sheffield.

Comedy Sketch, Take it From Here

He was a strong union man, my dad. When he read us a story at night, he'd say: 'Once upon a time and a half...'

Roy 'Chubby' Brown

An accountant is walking down the street and he's confronted by a poor old tramp who says, 'Give us a quid, I haven't eaten for three days.' The accountant says, 'Mmm, how does this compare with the same period last year?'

Barry Cryer

School

It was a tough school. The teacher said to the class: 'What comes after a sentence?' This kid says: 'You make an appeal.'

Stan Boardman

I used to get picked on quite a bit at school. I'd be walking down the corridor, people'd go, 'Oi, Speccy four eyes!' and I'd go, 'Er no, *two* eyes, *two* convex lenses. Think on, pal.'

Daniel Kitson

The thing about school was, I couldn't get my head around any of the prescribed books – 'The Hobbit' for instance... That's all we used to talk about – small men in holes.

Mark E. Smith, *Renegade*

The children of the working class...can join the offspring of the middle classes at the comprehensive schools and take comfort in the fact that they'll all come out equally uneducated.

Beryl Bainbridge, *English Journey*

Boarding school was wonderful and I fitted in perfectly. My only disappointment is that no one ever tried to bugger me. I feel that's a whole important part of growing up that I missed out on.

Jeremy Clarkson

I got expelled from Repton... It was just a collection of minor indiscretions, but it was a public school and you don't need to do that much to annoy them. Had I been at a high school back home in Doncaster, I'd have needed to rape the headmaster's wife and burn the place down to get thrown out.

Jeremy Clarkson

I recognise and acknowledge Eton's unique talent for getting stupid boys into Parliament.

Roy Hattersley

Far too many children have learning difficulties, induced by the fact that their teachers have teaching difficulties.

Keith Waterhouse

When I was at school, the boys all snogged Julie Miller in the art cupboard. They don't make teachers like Julie Miller any more.

Jason Manford

I was terribly badly behaved. Once we stripped a teacher down to her petticoat because we didn't like her.

Jilly Cooper

My father wanted me to have all the educational opportunities he never had. So he sent me to a girls' school.

Ken Dodd

As we read the school reports upon our children, we realise a sense of relief, that can rise to delight, that – thank Heaven – nobody is reporting in this fashion on us.

J.B. Priestley

There are so many things you learn in school that you never really need in real life: how an ox-bow lake forms; the boiling point of sodium; how to cover an exercise-book in flock wallpaper; how to play badminton in lost-property shorts.

Jeff Green

Knowing the chemical symbol for lead is of no use if you want to iron a blouse, or have sexual intercourse with a girl, or wire up a home cinema.

Jeremy Clarkson

—I wish I'd stuck in at school. It could have changed my whole life.
—That's true. You could be lying on the couch all day – with qualifications.

Andy and Flo Capp

University

—Would you like to go to university?
—Dunno. Maybe. I'd love to proper know about summat.

Interviewer and Alex Turner, frontman of The Arctic Monkeys

At first I was nervous, as a grammar schoolboy from the North of England, about contact with the public schoolboys... William Wordsworth in the original version of 'The Prelude' gave a picture of his first reactions to Cambridge in 1787, with which I can easily identify: '...I was the Dreamer, they the Dream; I roam'd delighted through the motley spectacle; gowns grave or gawdy, Doctors, Students, Streets, Lamps, Gateways, Flocks of Churches, Courts and Towers: Strange transformation for a mountain Youth, a northern Villager.'

Denis Healey, on going to study at Oxford

At Oxford we drank to ludicrous and revolting excess and threw up over some of the most beautiful buildings in Britain.

Steven Norris

Our tutor... asked us what poetry we knew by heart, pointing to me to begin. I was so discomforted that I just opened my mouth and out came 'Albert and the Lion' by Marriott Edgar.

Jeanette Winterson, at Oxford University

Oxford is a sexist little dump.

Jeanette Winterson

I went to Oxford University – but I've never let that hold me back.

Margaret Thatcher

[*talking to his teddy bear*] We're going to miss Cambridge, you and I, Hesketh – the cloister, the quad, those long afternoons in my rooms, the thwack of leather on Willow. Willow has promised to write, you know, but I don't believe he will.

Morris Hardacre, *Brass*

I never took to Cambridge and I don't think it ever took to me...
Cambridge society regarded me as a North-country lout of uncertain
temper. And now, fifty-five years too late, I realise that all those people
were quite right.

J.B. Priestley

There was a university in York when Oxford was just a place where cattle
walked across a muddy river, and the Venerable Bede taught Latin and
Greek in Jarrow when Cambridge was a couple of planks across a stream.

Roy Hattersley

Giz A Job: Unemployment

—Mister Capp, when was the last time you were in full employment?
—Do previous lives count?

Employment Agency Official and Andy Capp

I had to go to the Job Centre for a Restart Interview. It really bugs me cos
I am available for work. It's not my fault if there's no vacancies for a
netball coach.

Paul Calf, aka Steve Coogan

Has anybody seen that huge, pretentious advert outside the job centre?
Talk about aiming at the kids! It says: 'ARE YOU LOOKING FOR A JOB
INIT?' I went in and said, 'Oy, we're not all homeboys lookin' for nuf
respec. I've seen the poster outside, "ARE YOU LOOKING FOR A JOB
INIT?"' The bloke behind the counter said, 'It doesn't say that. It says,
"ARE YOU LOOKING FOR A JOB IN I.T.?"'

Lee Mack

Twelve hunting rifles; eleven spotty youths; ten fleas a-leaping; nine screaming babies; eight P45s; seven recovering alcoholics; six DMAs; five direct payments; four Fresh Starts; three crisis loans; two missed EVs, and a scally in a hoodie.

Alternative version of 'The 12 Days of Christmas' circulated by staff at a
Jobcentre in Birkenhead

I didn't mind being on the dole. I had a lot of time on my hands as a result. Other people went to university and I read books, smoked cigs and looked around most days. It's good to have a period like that in your life, when you're not being forced to think like others.

Mark E. Smith, *Renegade*

The great thing about being unemployed in the early Eighties was that you could devote yourself to the noble and sacred and artistic pursuit of Being Yourself... the fortnightly Giro was really an Arts Council grant.

Mark Simpson, *Saint Morrissey*

Perhaps governments, like proud old ladies who fail to take up their benefits, still think of social security as charity. Yet it is no more charity than the donation from the Civil List to the Royal Household.

Brian Redhead

My mother always supported me in an artistic sense, when many people around her said she was entirely insane for allowing me to stay in and write. It's this working class idea that one is born simply to work, so if you don't you must be of no value to the human race.

Morrissey

The trick to saving money on the dole was to minimise your life functions until they could barely be measured. This meant staying in bed for most of the day, while wearing two layers of clothes, with your overcoat over the bed to save fuel. In other words, you had to actually die, in an economical if not a clinical sense.

Mark Simpson, *Saint Morrissey*

I saw a good job advertised this mornin', Flo, so I went to see abaht it straight away. Yer start tomorrow.

Andy Capp

Graft: Work

Job Opportunities For Those With Earning Disabilities

Misprint in Headline, *The Preston Reporter*

My father said to me, 'I always wanted you to have the things in life I never had.' So he got me a job.

Roy 'Chubby' Brown

You'll be pleased to hear your father now has a new job, with 500 men under him: he's cutting the grass at the cemetery.

Ken Goodwin

You have to accept the treachery of the workplace. You cannot waste time discovering it daily. That's like saying every morning, 'Oh! Traffic in London.'

Anne Robinson

Hopefully, my daughter'll be a lawyer who doubles as a doctor – then she can fuck up operations and not be arsed about getting sued.

Noel Gallagher

Harriet Wrench breeds bulldogs, which amazes some people because bulldogs normally do it themselves.

Les Dawson

If you make one mistake, it's half a day out with the undertaker.

Fred Dibnah, steeplejack

The thing is nowadays, you'll have twenty men working, yet sixty men telling them, 'You can't do that, you ain't got a tin hat on!'

Fred Dibnah, steeplejack

My father was killed down t'pit in 1967. Terrible shock for me mother. He should never have been down there. He was a milkman.

Willis, *Brassed Up*

The only way blokes come home sooty-faced from work these days is if the toner cartridge had leaked while they were printing out their presentations on stock control innovation or the future of portable air conditioning.

Stuart Maconie, *Cider With Roadies*

Toughest job I ever had was working in a bank call-centre. The job was all right, it was the commute to Bangalore every day I couldn't handle.

Jeff Green

With sociology one can do anything and call it work.

Malcolm Bradbury, *Eating People is Wrong*

Architects are people who don't like fields.

Mike Harding, *The Armchair Anarchist's Almanac*

She's a stripper, my missus. She's on the roof right now, getting the lead.

Josh White

I sometimes dream about going back, but the DHSS is a bit like nuclear science. It's a fast-moving world, and once you lose touch with modern developments in social security legislation affecting persons working overseas, there's no catching up again.

Chris Donald, co-founder of *Viz*, on giving up his job at the DHSS

Find out why you were brought into this world, discover your talent, whatever it is. If you make sausages or daisy chains, make the best ones. That's the North-country ethic.

Patricia Routledge

I like to keep busy. As they say in Yorkshire, 'T'hardest wark is doing nowt.'

W.R. Mitchell

Brass: Money

What a great new year we're going to have! Everyone's been worrying about money. No need to worry about money any more. There isn't any.

Ken Dodd

As we're all painfully aware, this great nation of ours is going through a very severe economic depression. Not that a depression bothers me. Cos I was a failure during the boom.

Les Dawson

Never in the history of human credit has so much been owed.

Margaret Thatcher

[*pointing to his eyebrows*] I'm up to there in debt. I wish I was a bit taller.

'The Little Waster', aka Bobby Thompson

We call it 'debt', others call it 'credit', committee-men's wives call it 'on account'. Yeah, I'm in debt on account of not being able to pay my credit.

'The Little Waster', aka Bobby Thompson

Go and get measured for a suit, say, for £70, because you don't care what you spend when it's debt. They might want £5 a week. Don't pay. Wait till you get a summons from the County Court – £1 a month!

'The Little Waster', aka Bobby Thompson

People are spending more than they've got. It's become visible. I spotted it months ago. I saw a Bentley car in Dewsbury. Now, that's a £200,000 car – and Dewsbury itself is only worth £180,000.

Alun Cochrane

I just heard a credit card belonging to the wife has been stolen, but I am not going to report it. Turns out the guy who took it is spending a lot less on it than my wife used to.

John Prescott

I do wish I had brought my cheque book. I don't believe in credit cards.

Margaret Thatcher, visiting the Ideal Home Exhibition

I don't believe in hire purchase. Signing your life away. I've seen it 'appen too often before. People take on too much. Our Linda's husband, Geoffrey, he worked at Wainwright's, up on the estate, and they were really cracking it, plenty of overtime... and they went in for this hire purchase – new fridge, cooker, all this contemporary furniture, then what happens? There's a slump, isn't there – four-day week, no more overtime... Still got all the stuff to pay for. So, where are they? There they are, every night, watching a 23-inch television set on their Swedish sofa with their spin dryer and their cocktail cabinet, eating bread and marge. All they had in their fridge was ice cubes. That's the trouble with the country today – something for nothing mentality.

Terry Collier, *The Likely Lads*

There was a knock on the door last Thursday, 'Is Mr Thompson in?' Our lass says, 'Come in, take a seat.' He says, 'I'm coming in to take the lot!'

'The Little Waster', aka Bobby Thompson

I went to see the bank manager. He hopped into his office – well, he had to, I was kissing his feet at the time. In a jocular vein, I said, 'How does my account stand?' He said, 'I'll toss you for it.'

Les Dawson

Students: Left school? No job? No money? No prospects? Then fuck off.

Gnat West – the frank bank, advert, *Viz* magazine

Banks seemed to me to be glorified pawnbrokers. My parents kept their money under the sink. I had kept mine in a Tupperware box in the cistern.

Jeanette Winterson, on first opening a bank account at university

You couldn't borrow us a few quid, could ya? I've spent all me benefit money on me baby – 25 quid for one ear pierced! I've only got a fiver left, and that's fer his baby food.

Janice, *Early Doors*

Self-assessment? I invented that.

Ken Dodd

A country where it is impossible to live and nobody can afford to die.

Sir Thomas Beecham, on the British climate and death duties

To force myself to earn more money, I determined to spend more.

James Agate

Hang the expense and give the cat another kipper!

Jane Klemz, her grandfather's saying when considering a small extravagance

Mum gave Dad pocket-money for 26 years. Because he was so generous and financially inept, he couldn't be trusted with his own account... He got access to his bank account at the age of 55.

William, Alexandra, Tom and Florence on their dad, John Peel, read out at his memorial service

I've got my money in Lapland. That way I get frozen assets *and* I get to see Father Christmas.

Ken Dodd

The failure of the banks could have been predicted from the day they stopped putting blotting paper in cheque books.

Philip J. Barratt

An old Yorkshire lady who kept her money in a tin box, when advised to bank it because she was losing interest, replied: 'I put a bit extra in t'tin for interest every week.'

W. R. Mitchell

'Ow the 'eck d'you save for a rainy day when it tipples down six days a week?

Hilda Ogden, *Coronation Street*

—I started coming out to work to get some money behind me, but it just seems to disappear. Have *you* put anything aside?
—Yes, all thoughts of retirement.

Ruby White and Flo Capp

Spend, Spend, Spend! Rich

A friend of mine, Joan Deacon, swore if she ever won the pools it would not change her life one iota. Earlier this year she won £200,000 on the pools and immediately moved to Lytham St Annes. What a liar! It's not the winning. It's the barefaced hypocrisy that upsets me.

Mrs Merton, aka Caroline Aherne

Do you know that a lot of people who win the lottery end up with irritable bowel syndrome?

Marjorie Longdin, National Lottery winner and William Hague's auntie

—Will you benefit from your aunt's good fortune?
— We are a good Yorkshire family so I don't expect to see any of this money from Auntie Marjorie.

Reporter and William Hague

—Will you buy your wife a present?
—Maybe I'll let her have a look in the Argos catalogue.

Reporter and Terry Benson, £20 million lottery winner

You still have to worry about where the next Rolex is coming from.

Mel Eddison, self-made millionaire, commenting on his £2.5 million lottery win

People do similar things when they win the lottery: they buy houses, they buy cars, they go on holiday. But what I'd do, I'd go to my local box-office, I'd buy every single ticket for the next Mick Hucknall concert – and then just not bother going. Money well spent. Nobody there at his gig – or just me, like a weird stalker...

Jason Manford

We are always being told that the rich are getting richer. I don't know if this is true or not... What I *do* know to be true is that now there are more and more people who – in the North-country phrase – 'have more money than sense'. These people buy things just because they are expensive.

J.B. Priestley

Money can't buy happiness but, as my friend Lily points out, it can certainly buy alcohol.

Mrs Merton, aka Caroline Aherne

Charity

This woman came from the parish council, knocked on my door and said, 'We do a sponsorship every year. Would you like to get involved... It's a half-marathon.' I said, 'Oh, no, I couldn't do that – heel surgery.' She said, 'Well, think about it. It's for partially-sighted and blind children.' I thought, 'Fuck it, I could win that!'

Dave Spikey

Mean? You've never met a meaner man. He used to be a mountain-climber. He was trapped once, climbing the Matterhorn, frozen stiff to a ledge for two days and nights, hanging by his fingertips for grim death. They got a rescue helicopter a hundred feet below, a fella got out and shouted up, 'Ee y'are, Scouse, Red Cross!' He said, 'Clear off, I gave you tuppence last year!'

Tom O'Connor

—It used to be a tradition round here, if you were hungry you could knock on any door and without a moment's hesitation they'd slam it straight in your face!
—Well, what's that got to do with owt?
—Just shows they had character. Now we're into an age of compassion. The world's full of folk hating folk for hating folk.

Norman Clegg and William 'Compo' Simmonite, Last of the Summer Wine

This woman came to our house, she said, 'I'm collecting for the local swimming baths.' So I gave her a bucket of water.

Ken Goodwin

Tommy Cooper was doing a charity auction and he asked: 'What will you give me for this toaster?' My uncle John, who was in the audience, shouted: 'Two slices of bread!'

Les Dennis

Auction of Promises: Lot 7: a trip with the City of York's road gritting team.

York Evening Press

The best portion of a good man's life – his little, nameless, unremembered acts of kindness and of love.

William Wordsworth

No one would have remembered the Good Samaritan if he'd only had good intentions. He had money as well.

Margaret Thatcher

One seldom was able to do her a good turn without some thoughts of strangulation.

Alan Bennett, *The Lady in the Van*

A quick beggar story: a young man in Manchester... I was passing, and they all say the same thing, 'Have you got any change?' I hate that. When I was young, beggars were different. They used to tell you marvellous lies like: 'You're a great, handsome fella!' ...And then I'd give him two shillings. You bought the performance. You bought the lie, and then we are equals, and that's charming.

Tom Baker

—Knock, knock...
—Who's there?
—Biggish...
—Biggish who?
—Not today, thank you.

Peter Kay

A Penny Saved: Thrift

Did your mother scrape the paper the butter or lard was wrapped in, so as not to waste any?

Thora Hird

He's a right tight sod. He dropped 5p in the pub the other night and he was down that quick it hit him on top of the head.

Ken Dixon, *Early Doors*

Fred wasn't greedy at all, he just didn't like waste. He couldn't pass an elastic band without picking it up. If one broke, he'd tie a knot in it and use it again...[Amongst his possessions, he left] a packet of extra-strong mints, each of which he would cut into four. 'They're very expensive,' he'd say.

Obituary Notice of Fred Vasey, *The Northern Echo*

Save money at Christmas by returning last year's cards to the sender with the simple inscription: 'Same to you.'

Top tip, *Viz* magazine

I bought a bottle of Minadex for my father the day before he died. I was told it was supposed to do you good. If I had known what would happen I would have bought the smaller size.

Susan Fraser, overheard in Boots chemist, Sheffield

My husband and I save pounds every year on household wear and tear by living in a tent in the garden.

Top tip, *Viz* magazine

There must be thrifty ways to leave your lover.

Hovis Presley

Science and Technology

Science

Space isn't remote at all. It's only an hour's drive away if your car could go straight upwards.

Fred Hoyle

What a wonderful day it is for running down the road, sticking a green cucumber through the letter-boxes and shouting, 'The Martians are coming!'

Ken Dodd

If little green men land in your back yard, hide any little green women you've got in the house.

Mike Harding

—If you're an alien, how come you sound like you come from the North?
—Lots of planets have a north.

Rose Tyler and Dr Who, *Dr Who*

Two Geordies were arguing whether it was the sun or the moon they could see. Eventually, they turn to a passing Irishman. 'Paddy, is that the sun or the moon?' 'How should I know?' he replied, 'I'm a stranger 'round here.'

Anon

Apparently, if you stand on the Great Wall of China, you can see the moon.

Boothby Graffoe

I got a bit of moon rock once. When I broke it open it had 'moon' written all through it.

Ken Dodd

Computers and Technology

Isn't technology amazing these days? Take banking, for instance. Everything's so quick and computerised. They press a couple of keys and I can have my loan application rejected in seconds.

Andy Capp

I'm afraid email is a non-starter. I can't even use a bicycle pump.

Judi Dench

Sometimes you might think that the machines we worship make all the chief appointments, promoting the human beings who seem closest to them.

J.B. Priestley

Mechanical gadgets don't cut down the time spent, they just mean you wash sweaters after you've worn them once instead of scraping the food-blob off with your fingernail.

Jilly Cooper

Chat rooms are the new dinner parties. At least in the 70s you had to get up off your arse and go and meet these people, go around to their house...

Mark E. Smith, *Renegade*

I have to tell you that my relationship with techie stuff is about the same as my relationship with Scarborough – I know that decent people choose to live there, but I would rather not visit.

Jeanette Winterson

Me grandma was trying to wind a CD t'other night. First time she got a video, her and me grandad were in t'kitchen. I went in, and they were taping 'Gone with the Wind'... I said, 'Why don't you go and watch it?' She said, 'I will. I don't want to talk cos it'll come out on t'video.' You can just see it can't you: 'Frankly, my dear, I don't give a – Stan, d'you want a brew?' 'I'll think of some way to get him back cos after all, tomorrow is – Stan, yer tablet, yer tablet, it's 2 o'clock. Angina tablet!'

Peter Kay

The thing with high-tech is that you always end up using scissors.

David Hockney

Transport – General

I usually walk. It's the best way to get about, and people have been doing it for years. You see more as well.

Karl Pilkington

If God had meant us to walk everywhere, he wouldn't have given us Little Chefs.

Reverend Bernice Woodall, *The League of Gentlemen*

The problem with public transport is not the cost, geographical availability, frequency or efficiency of the services provided. It is the fact that a high proportion of people who use it smell.

M. Thigh, *Viz* magazine

All men who were men sat on the upper deck of the open tram in the invigorating sleet... Women sat inside, sniffing and looking at advertisements for Iron Jelloids and Owbridge's Lung Tonic. The driver had no windscreen-wiper, chiefly because he had no windscreen. Swathed in oilskins, purple-faced, he clung to the controls like the helmsman of a storm-wracked coffin ship.

E.S. Turner

They're all liars, taxi-drivers. We have a taxi-firm near me, I ring 'em up and say, 'Can I have a taxi, please.' They say, 'He's just turned your corner now.' I'm like, 'Can I order it first, before you start lying to me?'

Peter Kay

When you get in a taxi, you can't resist saying two things: ''Ave you been busy?' and 'What time are you on till?' *Why?* Why d'you do it? You can't help yourself!

Peter Kay

Cycling drunk is the closest you can get to flying.

Alexei Sayle

Oh, Mr Porter! Train

The industrial revolution which made England great was born and bred in the North. The event symbolising that explosion of ingenuity and energy was the first public steam train service. It ran from Stockton to Darlington, not Godalming to Guildford. It burst into life because Northerners were prepared to work hard at rough trades and dangerous jobs.

Roy Hattersley

This train will call at Garforth, East Garforth, Micklefield and Ulleskelf, due to arrive in York, whenever.

Guard's Announcement, Manchester to York train, 2000

If a train is late we will tut and sigh, working in pairs if possible. If an announcement is made to the effect that Cheshire and the North Midlands have been seized by a military dictator basing himself in Nantwich, we will look at our watches and say, 'There goes my Yogaerobics.'

Victoria Wood

207

Crewe has a great railway tradition. Even the pubs open ten minutes late.

Ken Dodd

The town of Crewe introduced one of the most famous phrases in the English language: 'Change at Crewe.' No matter where you bought your ticket, they'd always say, 'Change at Crewe.' Why they couldn't give you your change there I'll never know.

Ken Dodd

I believe that trainspotting was just one symptom of an underlying problem... Anoraxia, you might call it.

Chris Donald

—How long does it take to travel from London to Bath by train?
—Oh, a bottle of chardonnay. Leeds, my home town, takes a bottle-and-a-half. The good thing about that journey is that you can be drunk by Peterborough, hungover by Wakefield and sober by Leeds.

Unidentified Friend and Keith Waterhouse

On Sunday I took a train, which didn't seem to want to go to Newcastle.

J.B. Priestley

In the buffet on the steam train to Pickering, I engage two American tourists in conversation... She stares firmly out of the window. Unfortunately, at that point we are passing a white bottle bank on which someone had spray-painted a penis. I don't apologise; if it was in a Minoan cave everyone would think it was bloody marvellous.

Victoria Wood

Car

A copper pulled a fella up in his car. He said,' You know your wife fell out the car half a mile back.' The fella said, 'Thank God for that, I thought I'd gone deaf.'

Bernard Manning

—I saw your mother the other week – not to speak to, like, just through the car window.
—What car window?
—*My* car window.
—You mean to say you've got a car?
—Well, I haven't just got the window.

Bob Ferris and Terry Collier, *Whatever Happened to the Likely Lads?*

—Fast motor, is it?
—Like shit off a chrome shovel.

Ken Dixon and Phil, *Early Doors*

Skoda? Give over!

John Shuttleworth, aka Graham Fellows

I am slightly embarrassed by my enthusiasm for cars. I hide my car magazines inside porn.

Steve Coogan

David Frost has a convertible, open-top car. If it rains he just presses a button on the dashboard and – it stops raining.

Barry Cryer

If you're from Liverpool, by law, someone in your family *has* to have a van.

John Bishop

—What's the worst journey you've ever been on?
— I was stuck in the back of a car for two hours with Edwina Currie. We were going from London to Nottingham and the woman wouldn't stop rabbiting on... It was like being stuck with your mother-in-law.

Interviewer and Garth Crooks

A guy is driving down a country lane and he ran over a cockerel. He was very upset, and he went to the farmhouse and knocked on the door. A woman opened the door and he said, 'I appeared to have killed your cockerel; I'd like to replace him.' She said, 'Please yourself – the hens are round the back.'

Barry Cryer

I changed my sat nav to a bloke's voice cos the woman kept getting me lost.

Lee Mack

Motorists: always have a hot pie in your hands in heavy traffic. Each time the traffic grinds to a halt, just reach for the pie. The instant you place it to your lips the traffic begins to move.

Top tip, *Viz* magazine

A few weeks back, I was driving, and I really needed a wee – desperate I was. I was panicking, but I spotted an empty Coca Cola bottle in the passenger footwell so I thought, hold on a minute, I've weed before, I've driven before, how hard could this be together? So I started weeing in the bottle and it filled up pretty sharpish... but luckily it stopped 550 mls on the dot. I put the lid on and threw it out of the window. I know that's horrible but the worse thing was, he sat there, and he failed me for it.

Jason Manford

The wife's just passed her driving test. She said, 'I thought you'd get me something to run round in.' I said, 'I have – a tracksuit.'

Roy 'Chubby' Brown

Mirror. Check your lippy. Signal. Whistle at passing builder. Manoeuvre. Ask if he's free later.

Gennie Walker, learning to drive, *Emmerdale*

We were driving north back to Liverpool and we got past Birmingham, which always makes you feel better. I don't know why, you think you're nearly home, but you're not, you're miles away, but you still think you are...

John Bishop

Typical of the South, having traffic jams. We don't have them in the North. Well, there's no need for traffic in the North, is there? No one ever wants to go nowhere in the North. There's no one worth visiting in the North. You're best off stopping at home and counting the cat hairs on your cardigan.

Uncle Mort, *Uncle Mort's South Country*

Drivers: avoid getting prosecuted for using your phone while driving. Simply pop your mobile inside a large shell and the police will think you are listening to the sea.

Top tip, *Viz* magazine

In a crowded supermarket car park my husband and I were unable to find our car. We felt proper fools when, after three hours, we remembered we don't have one.

E. Rolands, *Viz* magazine

Jeremy Clarkson is like a 14-year-old boy trapped in a man's body. Not in the Gary Glitter way – obviously.

Jimmy Carr (F)

Clarkson on Cars

Think of the Alfa Romeo Brera as Angelina Jolie. You've heard she's mad and eats nothing but wallpaper paste. But you would, wouldn't you?

This is a Renault Espace, probably the best of the people carriers. Not that that's much to shout about. That's like saying, 'Oh good, I've got syphilis, the best of the sexually transmitted diseases.'

The Ferrari 355 is like a quail's egg dipped in celery salt and served in Julia Roberts's belly button.

I'd like to consider Ferrari as a scaled down version of God.

The air conditioning in Lamborghinis used to be an asthmatic sitting in the dashboard blowing at you through a straw.

Telling people at a dinner party you drive a Nissan Almera is like telling them you've got the ebola virus and you're about to sneeze.

The Mercedes CLS55 AMG sounds like Barry White eating wasps.

I would rather have a vasectomy than buy a Ford Galaxy.

Are cars as good as sex? There's no swelling when I climb into a car, unlike if I was, say, climbing into Claudia Schiffer.

Koenigsegg are saying that the CCX is more comfortable. More comfortable than what... being stabbed?

As something to live with every day, I'd rather have bird flu than the Covette Z06.

I've seen gangrenous wounds better looking than the Porsche Cayenne.

There are many things I'd rather be doing than driving the Porsche Cayman S, including waiting for Bernard Manning to come off stage in a sweaty nightclub, and then licking his back clean.

This car takes up less parking space than your average American tourist.

I'm sorry, but having an Aston Martin DB9 on the drive and not driving it is a bit like having Keira Knightley in your bed and sleeping on the couch. If you've got even half a scrotum it's not going to happen.

In a list of the five most rubbish things in the world, I'd have America's foreign policy at five. AIDS at four. Iran's nuclear programme at three. Gordon Brown at two and Maserati's gearbox at number one. It is that bad.

The seats in the Audi TT Convertible: there are footballers' wives who'd be happy with this quality of stitching on their faces.

The Zonda is like a lion in orange dungarees. Kind of fierce, but ridiculous all at the same time.

The highlight of my childhood – it's the Ladybird Book of Motor Cars... On page 40, you find the Maserati 3500 GT. Now this for me, when I was little, was kind of like Jordan and Cameron Diaz. In a bath together. With a Lightning jet fighter. And lots of jelly.

Racing cars which have been converted for road-use never really work. It's like making a hardcore adult film, and then editing it so that it can be shown in British hotels. You'd just end up with a sort of half-hour close-up of some bloke's sweaty face.

Bus

The other week a woman wearing a shocking pink shell suit, 50 if she was a day, got onto a bus in Huyton. 'Student card, lad,' she said to the driver, 'it's in me bag.' As dry as you like, he replied, 'Slow learner are you, love?'

Les Dennis

''Ere luv duz dis bus stop at the Pier 'ead?' 'Der'll be a bloomin' big splash if it duzn't!' the smiling driver said.

The Liverpool Saga

I don't understand bus lanes. Why do poor people have to get to places quicker than I do?

Jeremy Clarkson

The only time I've been on a bus in the last 25 years was when one stopped for me in Islington. The driver told me I had to get on so he could tell people he'd had Peter Stringfellow on his bus.

Peter Stringfellow

I cried all the way to Warrington until a man in a camel-hair coat got on to the coach and sat down next to me. He switched off the overhead light and covered both our laps with a plaid rug. He didn't speak to me. He interfered with me all the way to Knutsford and I was too polite to protest – it was quite kind, sharing the rug.

Beryl Bainbridge, on leaving Liverpool for London aged 16

Plane

I went to Dublin, three weeks ago, from Liverpool, for a pound. A pound! I didn't even want to go, to be honest with you. I was on my way to Blockbusters to get a DVD. I thought, I might as well save a few quid... I paid a pound for the seat, I ask for a cup o' tea on the plane – £2.50!

John Bishop

Liverpool Airport was renamed after the dead Beatle and given the new slogan: 'Above Us Only Sky'. I assume there's another one at the luggage carousel that says: 'Imagine No Possessions'.

Bill Leckie (F)

I hate airports. They get you there at 4 o'clock in the morning and keep you shopping for giant Toblerones till 10 o'clock at night.

Jenny Eclair

My old man was 67 before he went on an aeroplane. When I got a bit of money, I decided to send him and me mother on a plane. I rang up British Airways, and said, 'Fly them off first class, look after them...' When they came back, me mother said, 'Your father, he just lets me down! Do you know, he got so drunk on the plane, that after his meal, he offered to wash up.'

Michael Parkinson

—Dad, I've just been on Wikipedia, and I've discovered that Concorde used to fly at twice the speed of sound. In that case, how did they manage to speak to Air Traffic Control?
—In those days, Air Traffic Control would have been staffed primarily by women cos as you'll painfully discover in later life, they've got the ability to answer a question before it's been asked.

Justin Moorhouse Jr and Justin Moorhouse

Body, Mind and Soul

Appearance

My mother was looking through the window of our front parlour and my father said, 'Come away from there; people outside will think it's a pet shop.'

Eddie Braben, The Book What I Wrote

You've gorra face like a ruptured custard.

Scouse saying

I have a face like the behind of an elephant.

Charles Laughton, actor

I was in hospital in Lancashire after a car accident. The result was anything but pretty – my face was blue, red, yellow and purple and half as wide again as it should normally be. A woman visiting someone in the bed next to me bawled, 'Is it Thora?!' I nodded feebly. 'Eeee,' she continued, 'what a sight! I say, what a good job you were never good-looking before!'

Thora Hird

How lucky the lower classes are. They so seldom have beauty to lose.

Lady Patience Hardacre, Brass

Rita was a natural for every beauty contest where personality was not a factor.

Keith Waterhouse, Billy Liar

When I was in Dubai, I organised a Miss Wet Burka competition. You should've seen their faces!

Pauline Calf, aka Steve Coogan

then I saw her face, now I'm an amoeba

Hovis Presley, title of poem

I'm very fond of women, but in an orchestra if they're not good-looking – and often they're not and they always look worse when they're blowing – it puts me off; if they *are* good-looking it puts me off a damn sight more.

Sir Thomas Beecham

A good heart will help you to a bonny face, my lad...and a bad one will turn the bonniest into something worse than ugly.

Emily Brontë, *Wuthering Heights*

Don't I know your face from somewhere? Have you ever been a Peeping Tom?

Annie Brandon, *I Didn't Know You Cared*

My mother would say, 'I know he can't help his looks, but he could stop in.'

Margaret Wilson

We are never so attractive nor so repulsive as we often imagine ourselves to be. What we ignore is the idea that we may be just rather dull.

J.B. Priestley

You Can't See The Join: Hair

There's this notice in a hairdresser's in Liverpool: 'Beatles Haircut: 60 pence.' This fella went in; they cut all his hair off. He said, 'Eh pal, the Beatles don't 'ave their hair cut like this.' The hairdresser said, 'They do if they come in here.'

Bernard Manning

We call it 'her' in Liverpool. We always say, 'The Judy with the fer her.'

Ken Dodd

A word of advice regarding barbers: don't go to any barber with a pie shop next door.

Mike Harding, *The Armchair Anarchist's Almanac*

—Do you want beer, egg or herbal tonic?
—Nothing to drink, thanks.
—They're shampoos, you fool!

Hairdresser, Terry Collier and Bob Ferris, *Whatever Happened to the Likely Lads?*

What's that rubber mat thing hairdressers put around your neck? Excuse me, did ask for a saddle? You know what happens at the end of the day? They wipe that mat, then it goes back around the toilet.

Jeff Green

Don't let your wife cut your hair if you've got a temple to push down the next day.

Mike Harding, *The Armchair Anarchist's Almanac*

I never cut my hair. I wait till it drops out every autumn.

Uncle Mort, I Didn't Know You Cared

Alfred Wainwright was born with startling red hair; because nobody else in the family had red hair, he said he remembered as a baby being hidden in a drawer when visitors called.

Eric Robson, Outside Broadcaster

—Why did you grow a goatee beard?
—So I could be attractive to goats.

Reporter and Robbie Williams

Fashion

—Did you get that skirt from a catalogue?
—No.
—Pity, you could've sent it back.

Enid and Philippa, Dinnerladies

Never forget that what looks good on an 18-year-old fashion model in the catalogue is not necessarily right for a 66-year-old bookie's clerk from Chorley with elephantitus in her left knee.

Mrs Merton, aka Caroline Aherne

Listen lass, I've got to ask thee something. I lie in bed at night trying to figure it out. It's driving me crackers. I've got to know, Nora: are these stockings left hand thread or right hand thread?

William 'Compo' Simmonite, Last of the Summer Wine

I'm a martyr to piles, I am. I can't wear mini-skirts. Anything above the knee and they dip below the hem.

Jenny Eclair

—I wonder where Nora Batty were going all dressed up...
—I expect she was going to the doctor's. They always get dressed up to go to the doctor's. It's the only time that generation looks at all half smart is when they're half dead.

William 'Compo' Simmonite and Norman Clegg, Last of the Summer Wine

They tried to get me in a tracksuit once. They don't flatter.

Enid, Dinnerladies

My dress-sense is Yorkshire-prostitute-by-day casual wear, slightly unwashed.

Sara Cox

She's got the obligatory 'dobberwear' on – white leggings with a red thong. Every time she bends over a little bit of diamante keeps popping out the back: 'Babe'... She's more gold on than Mr. T, with the shittiest piece of jewellery ever designed – the jointy clown, the whole Elizabeth Duke at Argos back-catalogue's on this woman.

Dave Spikey

—My dress is vintage.
—So is my backside but I wouldn't want to show it in public.

Steph Stokes and Sadie King, Emmerdale

No one thought she had the courage. The nerve. Or the lingerie.

Tagline, Shirley Valentine

[*Compo is pegging out his greying long johns*] What the dickens is that you've got hanging up on the line – they look like a foggy day in Barnsley. You're not leaving washing like that out there in case some damn fool thinks it's mine.

Nora Batty, *Last of the Summer Wine*

I've put a new gusset in yer corset for you, Annie. And that's the last time! The next time you go up that ladder to paint that guttering, take yer corsets off – it's no wonder you got stuck on the overflow-pipe.

Les Brandon, *I Didn't Know You Cared*

I can remember when pants were pants. You wore them for twenty years, then you cut them down for pan scrubs.

Old Bag, *Victoria Wood, As Seen on TV*

You may mock. Wait till you get to my age. Me undergarments are the only things holding me together.

Blanche Hunt, *Coronation Street*

Men's legs must get very lonely in their trousers, standing in the dark all day.

Ken Dodd

Trousers, she now realised, were so designed not because their wearers had funny legs, but because men were constantly worried that an essential part of themselves might have gone missing. They wanted instant access, just to make sure things were in place. What was more puzzling was why they needed everyone else to check as well.

Beryl Bainbridge, *An Awfully Big Adventure*

—When I look at your wardrobe, I feel...
—Moist?

Trinny Woodall (F) and Jeremy Clarkson, What Not to Wear

[*Ken is wearing a silk kimono*] —Oh, for the love of God! A grown man dressed as a geisha! Have you gone stark staring mad?
—It's no different to a dressing gown. Is there a rule: 'Thou shalt wear terry towelling in the north west of England'?
—There should be.

Blanche Hunt and Ken Barlow, Coronation Street

Style is like the clap – you've either got it or you haven't. I've got it and now he has 'n' all!

Pauline Calf, aka Steve Coogan

I could never be like Pete Doherty and go out with dirt under my fingernails, a top hat on and my shirt hanging out. Working-class people take pride in their appearance.

Noel Gallagher

I don't dress weird cos people won't talk to you when you dress weird. I have this suspicion that only people who are very, very straight dress weird.

Mark E. Smith

—Aren't you cold like that?
—Oh, you mean the kilt?
—Yes. Put it on!

Ken Dodd and Scotsman (F)

So long as you can't see my genitals, I consider myself to be well-dressed.

Jeremy Clarkson

It doesn't matter how fat a bloke is, he wakes up in the morning, if it's a hot day, and thinks, 'I'll wear shorts!' Women don't do that. Women wake up in the morning, if it's a hot day, and think, 'Ooh, I'm too fat for shorts. I suppose I'd better put on something that makes me look clean, colourful and good with children.'

Jenny Eclair

It is a problem when you're overweight... I went into Burton's, the tailor's. I said, 'Have you got anything to fit me off the peg?' He said, 'Certainly. Try this tie on.' It was too tight.

Eddie Colinton

My mother has never had a cocktail dress for the simple reason that she has never had a cocktail.

Alan Bennett, *Telling Tales*

We take a rather wicked pleasure in being unfashionable.

Margaret Beckett, MP, on herself and husband Leo

When in doubt, overdress.

Vivienne Westwood

In a moment of stupidity I thought about getting meself some thigh-high boots and, fishing for a compliment, I said to my sister, 'Where would I get thigh-high boots that would fit *my* thighs?' And she said, 'Well, trannies must get them from somewhere.'

Sarah Millican

Our path led up Flintergill... Into view came a local farmer. He was wearing wellies – one green, one black. I commented that this was odd. Said the farmer: 'Nay – my lad's got a pair just same.'

W.R. Mitchell, *Yorkshire Post*

D'you remember going to school in a balaclava? Mine was all hard at the front where me dinner'd got on it. It's a wonder we're not deformed, the way our mothers used to send us to school to keep us warm. She used to put a pin through your underpants and balaclava and another at the back of your scarf. And that was in August.

Stan Boardman

Fred Dibnah's extraordinary cap seemed moulded with oil, age and, possibly, a steam hammer, to the consistency of a fried mushroom.

Nancy Banks-Smith

My cap's actually in my bag across the road in the barracks. It's really part of me. It's like a wig. I'm sure they would have asked me politely to remove it.

Fred Dibnah, on going to Buckingham Palace to receive the MBE from the Queen

Goodnight, sleep tight. Take yer cap off when you go to bed, love, or you'll not feel the benefit.

Annie Brandon, *I Didn't Know You Cared*

It's Grime Up North: Hygiene

It was inconvenient, Stella coming home and wanting a bath. As Uncle Vernon pointed out, it was only Wednesday.

Beryl Bainbridge, *An Awfully Big Adventure*

Bath twice a day to be really clean, once a day to be passably clean, once a week to avoid being a public menace.

Anthony Burgess

We used to have a bath in a tin bath – first the kids, then the whippets, then Grandad.

Ken Dodd

I can't abide showers. You can't do things in a shower what you can do in a bath. For a start off, in a bath, you can keep yer cap on while you cut yer toenails.

Uncle Mort, *I Didn't Know You Cared*

You had to cut up old newspapers and thread them on a string for the outdoor loo. When you were in there, you'd get a bit and start reading it, and then you couldn't find the continuation. My mother used to call out, 'You can stop reading – I've washed up!'

Thora Hird

It was on the toilet that I first read Freud and D.H. Lawrence, and perhaps that was the best place, after all.

Jeanette Winterson

What's Fer Tea? Food and Drink

Eee, I'm so hungry I could eat a horse between two bread-vans.

Bob Ferris, *Whatever Happened to the Likely Lads?*

—How long will dinner be?
—Four inches – it's a sausage!

Ernie Wise and Eric Morecambe

I'm that hungry, I could eat a nun's arse through the convent railings.

Lily Savage, aka Paul O'Grady

My wife's a rotten cook. Last year I bought her a pressure cooker. I don't know what she did, but she put a sprout in orbit.

Les Dawson

I can't see the point in making tons of food if people are just going to sit there and eat it.

Jenny Eclair

I went down to the snack bar and bought a bag of crisps. I got spring onion because I felt I needed to eat some vegetables.

Harry Pearson, *The Far Corner*

I think organic veg is just a fad – like vegetarian food or yo-yos.

Joan Bell, *Early Doors*

These potatoes are harder than the Kray twins.

Old Lady, eating 'Scouse', overheard by Ricky Tomlinson,
Ricky Tomlinson's Laughter Show

I'm on my third Aga, and if you love cooking you have to get one... There is no better way to dry your knickers and cook fish pie at the same time.

Jeanette Winterson

Until the cardboard tray is reintroduced to the Bounty bar, I'm not interested, and until Snickers reverts to its name of Marathon, I'll give them a wide berth.

John Shuttleworth, aka Graham Fellows

I eat a third of a Mars Bar a day – just to help me rest.

John Cooper Clarke

Is bottled water worth it? I can tell you now, No. You can get water that's passed through an iceberg, water that's passed through a glacier, water that's passed through Tasmania... At those prices it'd have to have passed through Barbra Streisand before I'd drink it.

Paul O'Grady

—I fancy a bag o' crisps!
—Ooh, what flavour?
—Prawn cocktail.
—Ooh, you posh git!

Sandra and Tracey, *Fat Slags*

You don't know anything about food – avocado pear with custard!

Bob Ferris, *The Likely Lads*

Garlic bread – it's the future. I've tasted it.

Brian Potter, *Phoenix Nights*

I like food. Always provided it isn't interfered with.

Uncle Mort, *Uncle Mort's South Country*

227

If I had the choice between smoked salmon and tinned salmon, I'd have it tinned. With vinegar.

Harold Wilson, prime minister

In 'Coronation Street', Fiz invited Roy to share her tuna bake (not a euphemism but an inferior form of fish pie from Freshco).

Nancy Banks-Smith

Accrington in the 1960s was not on the gourmet trail. As a child, my relationship to food was simple: eat it hot now or cold later. Whatever was left over at dinner time – old-fashioned 12 o'clock for us – was returned at teatime dressed in salad cream. Whatever survived the salad cream was suffocated between two slices of bread and plated up with a pickle for supper.

Jeanette Winterson

I grew up with a mother who wouldn't let me have a drink with soup cos 'soup's a drink *and* a meal – now get on with it!'

Lucy Mangan (F)

—Eat your dinner! There are millions of children starving in Africa who would love to have your food.
—Name one!

Sally and Sophie Webster, *Coronation Street*

Southern friends would go home to their southern parents who'd say: 'What do you want for tea, darling?' I'd get home and my mum would say: 'Right, what d'you want? It's mince or it's mince.'

Lucy Mangan (F)

I've had that much corned beef, if anybody cracks a whip, I'm away at a gallop.

'The Little Waster', aka Bobby Thompson

Last time I went home, me mam were ill in bed, poorly. I said, 'It's all right, mam, leave everything to me.' She said, 'I can't. It's baking day today.' I said, 'I'll look after that.' I went in the kitchen, got 9lbs of flour, 9lbs of yeast, some salt, some water, mixed it all together, and bunged it in the oven. About half an hour after, she shouts downstairs, 'Have you got that bread in the oven yet, Ted?' I said, 'Got it in the oven? It's tekkin' me all me time t'keep it in t'blinking kitchen!'

Ted Lune

'Farmhouse Kitchen'... Who can forget the grim-faced dead ringer for Mrs Squeers, miserably pounding lard in a bucket, studding it with dried fruit, and calling it Sad Cake?

Jeanette Winterson

I remember being absolutely amazed by shop-bought cake. I used to crave things like Mr Kipling's – brightly-coloured cakes that weren't badly iced, because my mother used to make her own cakes. There was always a fruitcake in the pantry – sometimes they were a bit dry, and my father used to say, 'Oh, it's a bit of a Gobi,' because it was as dry as the desert.

Jenny Eclair

Pontefract cakes like the buttons on an undertaker's coat.

Eric Sykes, *If I Don't Write It, Nobody Else Will*

We ate a lot of rice pudding – Mother would put a pint of milk into a pudding and bake it in the oven with a grating of nutmeg and a flavouring of vanilla. Does that make your mouth water? It does mine.

Ernie Wise

I've found me favourite shop. It's Greggs the bakers. Why is it that the front window is always full of gingerbread men? Thousands of 'em. Nobody ever buys 'em. Not even fat people. I reckon these gingerbread men are at it – they're reproducing and just keep piling up. At Christmas, Greggs panic: 'We've got thousands of 'em, what are we going to do?' 'I know! Stick a red hat on, blob of icing for a beard and it's Santa Gingerbread man!'

Justin Moorhouse

'Dobbers' have had that many Greggs pastries, they stink of pastry. If Jamie Olivier ever went round their house to sort out their eating habits, they'd just put a crust on him.

Dave Spikey

I'm partial to a cheese and onion pasty... I have often said I would like to be the face of Greggs.

Milla Jovovich (F), model, the face of L'Oréal

—These are vegetarian pasties.
—Lovely – and have you put much meat in them?

Unidentified baker and Margaret Thatcher

My mam made us laugh. We'd come down on a morning, she'd be doing the breakfast in her slippers. Me father said, 'I must get her a frying pan.'

Roy 'Chubby' Brown

The other morning, the wife gave me breakfast in bed. It slid off the plate when she threw it. I didn't mind. There was something strangely erotic about poached egg on quilt.

Les Dawson

I like a Blackpool breakfast, me – 20 ciggies and a pot of tea.

Lily Savage, aka Paul O'Grady

Tea, Ern?

Eric Morecambe, to Ernie Wise

This tea's very strong. Don't poke the bag so hard next time, I'm not a removal man.

Dolly, *Dinnerladies*

The Yorkshire Pudding was originally baked to be used as an edible 'carrying crust' or pouch... it would be folded over like a folded flat cap to carry cold roast beef and vegetables to the field. In fact, once dried and hardened, they offer much the same protection as caps and were sometimes worn upside down on the head on remote hill farms in Yorkshire with the front pulled out like a peak. Some people believe that flat caps actually started life this way.

Simon Thackray, *Yorkshire Post*

My father was a big Yorkshire offal-eater. He used to eat all the valves and pipes and innerds. I'd come home from school: 'Mark, nip down to t'butcher's and pick up some pig's nasal-passages fer yer dad's tea.' You couldn't go for a walk with me dad. If you went past a bad accident, 'Eh, that looks tasty!'

Mark Hurst

When the cow heel pie was cooked, my little brother used to suck on the cow's heel to help him with his teething.

Unidentified Northerner

Every cottager kept a pig in those days, and when the pig was killed hams and flitches of bacon hung from the ceiling in the kitchen, and dishes were filled with brawn, fried pig-cheek, boiled pig-nose... and there was always an eager group of boys waiting for the bladder which was blown up and hung to dry; they made grand footballs.

Mary Fenton

There has never been anything to touch a well boiled, heavily seasoned Black Pudding. As a weapon of defence it can acquit itself with honour and make an opponent reel in a comatose state; but to digest... ah! Steamy, ebon and fatty, it is at its most noble when swilled down with a pint of Old Peculiar.

Les Dawson

My dad told us that black puddings lived at the bottom of the garden, like they were little animals. Every morning he'd go down, catch a few in a net, take their legs off, poke their eyes out, put 'em in a pan and have 'em for his breakfast... No wonder I got bullied at school: 'What you doing this weekend, Jas?' 'Goin' black pudding hunting with me dad!'

Jason Manford

Our friends in the South employ the pudding as shorthand for the grim earthiness they imagine characterises the North. What they should know is that Homer tells of Agamemnon and his fellows feasting on black pudding outside Troy: such is the ancient tradition followed by the heroes of Yorks and Lancs.

Charles Nevin

I was about 18, and I went to London with work for the first time. They said, 'We're going to take you out for dinner,' so at about one o'clock I sat waiting for them. I rang them up and said, 'I thought we were going out for dinner?' and they said, 'Yeah, 7 o'clock, mate,' and I went, 'What? Fer yer *dinner*?'

Justin Moorhouse

Don't be late, I'm making takeaway for tea!

Flo Henshaw, *Two Pints of Lager and a Packet of Crisps*

Chips With Everything: Fish and Chips

A Scouser walked into a fish and chip shop with a 20lb salmon under his arm. He went, 'Eh, lad, d'you do fish cakes?' He went, 'Yeah.' He said, 'Can you do one for Thursday, it's his birthday.'

Mickey Finn

—This is one of the great meals of the world, fish and chips, and the British invented it.
—In the dark days, when Britain was in the throes of depression and unemployment...
—You mean last Christmas?
—I mean, the 1930s, before the war, that's when the fish and chip shop was invented. And it saved the poorer people, because it meant the working classes could get a hot meal a day.
—Right. And don't tell me there isn't any nutrition in it because if our parents' generation was brought up on this in the 30s, they didn't do so bad in the 40s.

Terry Collier and Bob Ferris, *Whatever Happened to the Likely Lads?*

233

When I was a little kid in Wigan, seemingly everyone went to the chippy on a Friday night... Some took bowls with them, the sort you might put on a child's head to help with a cheap haircut, and asked for them to be filled with chips, which they'd take home covered with a tea towel. (We didn't do this because my mum thought it was common.)

Stuart Maconie, *Pies and Prejudice*

—I'll 'ave cheese and onion pie, sausage and chips, peas and gravy and three fish, please.
—Bloody 'ell... I bet even Jesus'd struggle with this fish order.

Customer in Fish and Chip Shop and Bob 'Bing' Crosby, *Sunshine*

Chip Butty: Spread at least four layers of best butter on a thick slice of fresh bread, then add a heap of hot greasy chips, press another slice of well-buttered bread on top, and dig in. Swill down with a mash of fine tea brewed in a copper kettle.

Les Dawson, recipe

Pudding and chips on a tray with gravy – the only meal I miss now I'm a vegetarian.

Victoria Wood

A man who is sick of chips is tired of life.

Cilla Brown, *Coronation Street*

The Northern chip is a big chip. It's the kind of chip that if you drop it, you've actually lost something.

Jenny Eclair

Who could possibly respect a part of the country [the South] where they can only eat fish and chips with the aid of a little wooden fork? If God had meant us to eat la-di-da, he would not have given us fingers.

Roy Hattersley

Them fancy London types don't know the pleasure of eating chips with fingers.

Fred Dibnah, steeplejack

'Cheap as chips' – what sort of a saying is that? How much are chips round your way? They're 90p in my village – that's 18 bob in old money. If I went to t'chippy when I was a kid and said, 'Can I have 18 bob's worth of chips,' they'd have shut down! There wouldn't have been enough potatoes in Bolton for 18 bob's worth o' chips.

Dave Spikey

You've got to take that job in the chippy. It's perfect. Bottom of the road so no bus fares, and we won't 'ave to buy a single meal so no food bills, and the thought of you smelling of chip-fat morning, noon and night – what a turn-on that would be!

Les Battersby to Cilla Brown, *Coronation Street*

—Chip, Stu?
—Ta, where are they from?
—Greasy Lil's.
—Oh no, Greasy Lil's are horrible. Why didn't you go to Benthams?
—Well, you see, Greasy Lil's *are* horrible. But you get more chips there.

Stuart Maconie, *Cider With Roadies*

—You can stick yer Michelin stars where the monkey keeps his bad nuts. You'll not beat these fish and chips.
—No one makes good old-fashioned *English* fish 'n' chips like the Chinese.

George and Bob 'Bing' Crosby, *Sunshine*

Restaurant

A man rang his friend and said, 'Oh, I've been to a fabulous restaurant – the music, the ambience, the food, the service – fabulous!' His friend said, 'What was it called?' He said, 'It was called the er – oh, what's the name of that tall, thin thing with thorns and a flower on the top?' His friend said, 'A rose?' He said, 'Rose! What was the name of that restaurant we went to?'

Maureen Lipman

—Marion went out for a meal last Friday with her husband, Lionel. They both had *à la carte*. What is *à la carte*?
—I don't know. I wouldn't mind trying *à la carte* one night, I'm sick of chops.

Nana and Barbara, *The Royle Family*

[*eating nouvelle cuisine*] —By 'eck, you don't get much, do you?
—It's very well presented though.
—Aye, so's *Blue Peter*.

Eric Gartside and Shelley Unwin, *Coronation Street*

—There was hardly anything on his plate. Did you see his bean sprout?
—It's a wonder he's got the energy.

Cissie Braithwaite and Ada Shufflebottom, aka Roy Barraclough and Les Dawson

The meal was pretentious — a kind of beetroot soup with greasy croutons; pork underdone with loud vulgar cabbage, potato croquettes, tinned peas in tiny jam-tart cases, watery gooseberry sauce; trifle made with a resinous wine, so jammy that all my teeth lit up at once.

Anthony Burgess

The strangest meal I've eaten was in China where I ordered by pointing at the indecipherable dishes on the menu. When the meal came, the centrepiece was a whole pigeon battered in an upright position.

Ross Noble

People assume that because you've eaten bull's penis or grasshoppers, they must be the worst things you've ever eaten – but more disgusting were those huge plates of food they give you in America. Totally tasteless.

Michael Palin

—Do you want the ten and sixpenny luncheon or the half crown special?
—The half crown special will do.
—Right you are. It's the same thing only I've got to take these flowers off the table.

Richard 'Stinker' Murdoch (F) and Arthur Askey

For her starter, she had soup of the day, which was Friday.

Nana, *The Royle Family*

The Anglo-Saxon view of a banquet can be expressed in terms of the history of the world. You begin with soup – water with things swimming in it – then move on to the aqueous kingdom, then to flying creatures, then to mammals. Finally you celebrate man in cheeses and desserts, both products of sophisticated culture.

Anthony Burgess

I rang a takeaway last night. I said, 'Do you deliver?' They said, 'No, we do lamb, chicken and fish.'

Peter Kay

The curry was like a performance of Beethoven's Ninth Symphony that I'd once heard played on a player and amplifier built by personnel of the Royal Electrical and Mechanical Engineers, especially the last movement, with everything screaming and banging 'Joy.' It stunned, it made one fear great art. My father could say nothing after the meal.

Anthony Burgess

I don't know what you were eating last night but your breath has singed the bloody pillow. You've burned all the varnish off the bed-head... I've had to get up four times in the night to put the bloody wallpaper out. By 'eck, are your guts bad! You've 'ad the duvet across the room seventeen times! You've 'ad the ships answering back from Salford Docks. They've launched the Morecambe lifeboat twice. And there's sixteen factories round 'ere clocked off six hours early.

Mike Harding, after a curry

I only eat in someone else's restaurant if I'm thinking of buying it.

Marco Pierre White

Fat and Thin

I put weight on about 8 years ago, and I was looking forward to it because I genuinely thought that if I became fat I'd become bubbly and get a great personality. All I ever heard about fat people is how nice they were. But I'm not. And I'm still miserable. I just eat chocolate at two in the morning and cry.

Mick Ferry

Me nana was really huge. She always used to say: 'I've just got to walk past a cream cake shop and I put weight on,' yet in her bag she always had an emergency pasty.

Sarah Millican

—I thought you said she had a million-dollar figure.
—She has, but it's all in loose change.

Ernie Wise and Eric Morecambe

Come into the front parlour, and mind your hips on the ornaments – this hall can be very tricky for women of your build.

Pat Brandon, *I Didn't Know You Cared*

You can always get a fuck off a fat girl. Just throw a Mars Bar on the bed.

Roy 'Chubby' Brown

Somebody said to me recently, 'Are you pregnant?' I said, 'Only if I've been fucked by Mr. Kipling.'

Sarah Millican

It's easy to distract fat people. It's a piece of cake.

Chris Addison

I've noticed recently how you can tell, as a woman, whether or not you're overweight. It's during the throes of passion, when your partner picks you up, whether or not he says, 'One, two, three!' first.

Sarah Millican

They all think Wayne's a big fat person and eats burgers every day, which he's not... It does my head in because people really believe that. His favourite food is lettuce.

Coleen Rooney

I feel bad about always taking the mickey out of Fat Bob for being fat. But he got his own back on me at his funeral cos I carried the coffin. Nearly gave me a hernia.

Paul Calf, aka Steve Coogan

I've never been the same fellow since my old missus passed away. Twenty-two stone she weighed – a fine figure of a woman she was. I had her cremated. I went round a day or two later for the ashes. The fellow said to me, 'We've no ashes for you, but there's four buckets of dripping you can have.'

Frank Randle

Diet and Exercise

We have massive involuntary euthanasia in the UK and it's called 'Living in the North.'

Dr Phil Hammond (F)

—I'm all for healthy eating: sausage, egg, bacon, black pudding and fried bread.
—That's not healthy eating!
—It is if you leave the window open.

Morecambe and Wise

The last time I tried dieting, the only place I lost weight was my feet.

Eric Pickles, MP

I spoke to a doctor who said what John Prescott was suffering from was Münchhausen's Bulimia by Proxy: he did all the eating and other people were sick around him.

Fred MacAulay (F)

Yoga... aerobics... Pilates... they keep coming up with new names for looking stupid in leotards.

Andy Capp

My gym's not full of posers in thong-leotards. Everybody looks like me... Nobody could cope with a thong-leotard. In fact, for a high-impact class, a lot of us wear Pampers.

Victoria Wood

—I can't understand anyone jogging when, with a little extra effort, they could chase Nora Batty.
—What would worry me is, what would you do if you caught her?

William 'Compo' Simmonite and Norman Clegg, *Last of the Summer Wine*

The wife's doing yoga. Apparently, it's good for your body, but you have to lie completely naked on the floor and get your legs right behind your head. Well, I don't know. I walked in the bedroom, I went, 'Oh, will you comb your hair and put your teeth in, you're looking more like your mother every day.'

Roy 'Chubby' Brown

I swim like a fish – a cooked one.

Maureen Lipman

Andy isn't keen on swimming. The water gets into his beer can.

Flo Capp

Keep On Tekkin' The Tablets: Health

—Oh, hello, Ann. How lovely to see you again. And how's John now?
—Well, he still has to stand sideways.

R. Mahoney, overheard at a Sheepdog trial in the Peak District

I've got a really sore neck. Flo asked me to paint the kitchen ceiling today
– and I think I damaged it shaking my head.

Andy Capp

I don't feel very well. In fact, if I put me mind to it, I could be very ill indeed.

Cissie Braithwaite, aka Roy Barraclough

I'm blessed with a robust constitution, my father's mother ran her own
abattoir, and I've only had the need of hospitalisation once – that's when I
was concussed by an electric potato peeler at the Ideal Home Exhibition.

Kitty, *Victoria Wood, As Seen on TV*

—I've got high blood pressure and water retention – d'you know what
that gives you?
—Boiling water?

Sheila Openshawe and Bren, *Dinnerladies*

Me, I'm 82, as full of vim as a butcher's dog and as lively as a cricket. Why, I'll take anybody on of me age and weight, dead or alive... and I'll play 'em at dominoes!

Frank Randle

I'm as fit as a Rawtenstall flea.

Bradley Hardacre, *Brass*

Irritable bowel syndrome, that's just become a status symbol that has. This has all come in in the last ten years. What happened to flatulence, by the way? That never seems to get a look in.

Dolly, *Dinnerladies*

—He has great difficulty in passing water.
—Can't he move inland?

Nora Batty and Norman Clegg, *Last of the Summer Wine*

I miss proper chemists... I remember, years ago, I had a swollen finger filled with pus and the local chemist said, 'Go home, do some washing and have the water as hot as you can bear.' Sensible and it worked. These days you have to be sold something.

Liz Smith

My nan was complaining of chest pains. I said, 'Are you all right, Nan?' She said, 'I think I've got vagina.'

Peter Kay

A man was told his wife was sick, and that she either had AIDS or Alzheimer's – they weren't sure which. He asked a friend if he could offer any advice. The friend suggested: 'Take her to a remote part of the country, somewhere where she's never been before, and drop her off. If she finds her way home...don't fuck her.'

John Cooper Clarke

The best thing about having Alzheimer's is you never have to watch repeats on TV.

Mark Heath

Doctor

A bloke went to the doctor's, he's got a steering-wheel stuck in his underpants. The doctor says, 'That looks painful.' He says, 'It's driving me nuts.'

Dave Spikey

He can't stand pain – even when it doesn't hurt.

Pearl Sibshaw, Last of the Summer Wine

[*in the waiting room*] —It's going to be a long wait. There's a broken collarbone in there at the moment. Then there's this gentleman.
—I shan't be long.
—You never know, do you? Might be worse than you think. You don't look too clever to me.
—I've only come for the wife's prescription.

Terry Collier and Elderly Gentleman, Whatever Happened to the Likely Lads?

All I wanted was a sick note for a day off work. The doctor could see there was nothing wrong with me – and he made me strip right off. I wouldn't care, but I'd only washed for a stiff neck.

Al Read

Our doctor's friendly... I went with a headache, and he said, 'Take your clothes off.' I said, 'Where should I put them?' He said, 'Over there, on top of mine.'

Eddie Colinton

My mother would never encourage us to go to the doctor if we were ill... cos she said you should put up with everything, which is a very Northern thing – you don't show your emotions, you don't show that you mind about anything.

Victoria Wood

Good God, you don't go and see a doctor about serious symptoms. Struth! He might tell you you'd got a fatal illness – you'd drop down dead with terror.

Uncle Mort, *I Didn't Know You Cared*

The doctor said, 'Will you bring a stool-sample in?' I'm not sitting on the bus with a turd in me handbag. Disgusting. Say you forget it's in yer bag, wrapped up nicely in a serviette, and you go to a posh function six months later, and someone says, 'Can I borrow your hankie?' 'Yes, here you are.' 'Aagh!'

Lily Savage, aka Paul O'Grady

They said, 'We'll have to do an internal examination, do you mind if we bring in 16 students?' I said, 'Well, it depends what they're students of. If it's mechanical engineering, yes, I do mind.'

Victoria Wood

If it's a second opinion you want, I could come back tomorrow.

Dr McDuff (F), *Brass*

Dentist

We had to go to the dentist. I said, 'Don't fuck about, I haven't got time. No gas, no needle, just yank it out.' He said, 'Chubby, you must be a bit of a hard case. We get a lot of big babies in here. Which one is it?' I said to the wife, 'Show him your tooth.'

Roy 'Chubby' Brown

The best way to avoid having a dentist hurt you too much is to take a small revolver with you.

Mike Harding, *The Armchair Anarchist's Almanac*

The woman next door has had all her teeth taken out and a new fireplace put in.

Ted Lune

Hospital

I arrived in Manchester and drove past 'Hope Hospital'. Is this really the best name for a hospital? Hope is the last resort. When there's nothing else, there's always hope, and you name your hospitals this? 'Hiya, I'm here to see me dad.' 'Right, you need the "Fingers-Crossed Unit", that's straight down there. If you get to "50-50 Ward" you've gone too far.'

Michael McIntyre (F)

I spent four and a half hours in casualty with my 13-year-old son, Derek, who came back from his Halloween party early with third-degree burns, bobbing for chips.

Dave Spikey

Hospital patients: Arrive for your appointment two hours after the assigned arrival time. That way, you will only have to wait an hour for your doctor to see you.

Top tip, *Viz* magazine

A few months after our little boy, Andrew, arrived, my elder son, Robin, was due to go into hospital to lose his tonsils. He was very brave. He said to his mother, 'I'm not afraid of going into hospital, Mum. I'll take my medicine, but I'll tell you one thing: I'm not going to let them palm off a baby on me like they did on you. I'm going to hold out for a puppy.'

Ted Ray

When I was younger I was in the three-legged race, and I tripped and fell. I broke my ankle, actually tore it in half. I was rushed to hospital, it went gangrenous and they had to amputate, so, now, I've only got two legs.

Nick Margerrison

When I was in hospital, they treated me with the latest wonder-drug – Phenolacetaterictofolicideantibogitateamabatiful. Wonder-drug they call it! Honestly, it's just good old Epsom Salts with a publicity agent.

Ted Ray

My father was given suppositories. 'These pills are so useless,' he told the nurse, 'I might as well shove them up my arse.'

Andrew Metcalfe

The food's terrible. They're always trying to make me eat boiled fruit. I said to that nurse, I said, 'It's all right for them as like it; I like summat as 'as looked over a wall.'

Ena Sharples, *Coronation Street*

—You know who else is poorly? Norma Tittershall's husband, John. They don't think he'll come out of hospital. She says he's just lying there waiting for the end. She was on her way to the hospital when I bumped into her.
—Oh dear. What would you find to talk about in a situation like that?
—I don't know. She says she just sits by his bed and reads him his horoscope.

Winnie Cooper and Jean Dixon, *Early Doors*

When the doctor was there, Alfred refused to believe that he'd had a stroke. 'I can't have had a stroke,' he grated, in a terrible rage, 'I've got £93,000 in my current account.'

Tom Baker, *Who on Earth is Tom Baker?*

Ken Dodd went in for open-heart surgery. They opened him up and found another forty grand.

Jimmy Tarbuck

I was working on casualty one day. I said, 'Doctor, you're not gonna believe what I've just seen out there.' He said, 'What?' I said, 'There's three black fellas out there, and one of them's got a white willy.' He said,

'Never!' I said, 'Go and have a look.' He came back, he said, 'You soft cow! They're all miners – one's been home for his dinner.'

Pauline Daniels

When are you going to chuck up this lark and come and look after me, Nurse Gladys? Nursing is no profession for an 'andsome lass. I mean, I fancy the uniform, yes, but it's never knowin' where yer hands 'ave been.

Arkwright, *Open All Hours*

Visiting the Sick

'Ello, I 'eard you weren't very well. I thought I'd just come and cheer you up a bit. You're not looking too well, are you? I've brought you some flowers. I thought if I was too late, they'd come in 'andy, but I see you're still 'ere.

Auntie Doleful, aka Norman Evans

—We've bought you some grapes... Aren't you going to eat them?
—Not now. A bit later.
—Suit yourself, only don't leave it too long – you do look bad, don't you? Eh, I'm glad I didn't give my black coat away.

Lily Tattersall and Eli Pledge, *Nearest and Dearest*

You what? You're feeling a lot better? Ah, well, y'never know. There was Mrs White at Nob Hill last Thursday, you know, she was doing nicely, just like you are, y'know, and all of a sudden she started with spasms round the heart and she went off like a flash of lightning on Friday. They're burying her today. I thought of going up but, nah, I thought I'll pop in and cheer you up. You're looking a lot worse than what you were when I first come in.

Auntie Doleful, aka Norman Evans

Try and smile a bit and look cheerful, ooh, I'll tell you what, Mrs Jones on t'next street, she's on t'last lap, you know. She's got what you 'ave – there's no hope at all.

Auntie Doleful, aka Norman Evans

Always try to keep a smile on your face, and then if you 'appen to pop off suddenly, you'll make a nicer corpse.

Auntie Doleful, aka Norman Evans

Suicide

I was once with my mum and dad...in Airedale hospital near Keighley and my mother was being treated for depression. There's a long central corridor in this hospital, and in the dead hour of the afternoon we were walking down this corridor, which was empty, except for a woman who was coming very slowly towards us. As we drew nearer, my mum said, 'You see this woman walking down here? She's tried to commit suicide three times.' [*to the woman*] 'Hello!'

Alan Bennett

—If you want to end it all, drowning – now, there's a way to go.
—I can't swim.
—Well, you don't have to fuckin' swim, you divvy, that's the whole point. God, you're not very keen are you?

Dave and Lomper, *The Full Monty*

A small crowd had gathered. They were looking at the top of a tall building. A man stood on the edge of the roof and was threatening to throw himself off. I joined the crowd and a woman next to me turned to another woman and said: 'If he doesn't hurry up I shall miss my bus.'

Richard Whiteley

Are You Putting It Around That I'm Barmy? Madness and Therapy

It's ten years since I went of out my mind. I'd never go back.

Ken Dodd

I have kleptomania, but when it gets bad, I take something for it.

Ken Dodd

Sigmund Freud...had a one-track mind and a sewer mentality. He was the Roy 'Chubby' Brown of his day, but never as funny.

Mrs Merton, aka Caroline Aherne

Who thinks Freud is how Brummies like their eggs?

Anne Robinson, *The Weakest Link*

Spare a thought for my friend Eliza Hamilton, who was wrongly diagnosed as mentally unstable when all she was was a bit giddy.

Mrs Merton, aka Caroline Aherne

She were agoraphobic for six months till they 'ad that chip pan fire at home and then she were first one out the house.

Debbie, *Early Doors*

It's the American hippies' fault, they saw an in there, a way of making money out of bad moods. That's all it is most of the time. You can't expect to feel cock-a-hoop every minute of the day. My mam and dad's generation understood this.

Mark E. Smith, *Renegade*

Stress is a condition that the unstressed do not have a lot of time for... You never used to hear of council school teachers or the district nurse or the village bobby being off with stress, and we managed to get through the Blitz without stress counsellors.

Keith Waterhouse

Counselling? My mother was trapped under a Blackpool tram for four and a half hours, she didn't get counselling! She got a cup of tea and two tickets to Charlie Drake.

Dolly, *Dinnerladies*

—Here I am, suffering from an emotional crisis, and all you can say is, 'Eat yer chips!'
—That's the soundest advice you'll ever get for an emotional crisis, is that. There's all those over-privileged, neurotic, society women, at this very moment lying on psychiatrists' couches, and the best thing for them'd be a plateful o' chips.

Granville and Arkwright, *Open All Hours*

My dad's 83, and he phoned me the other day to say he'd had his first bout of depression. He said it was like all the lights in the world had gone out and he couldn't see the point any more. I said: 'How long did it last?' He said: 'An hour and a half.' Then he snapped out of it and did the cryptic crossword.

Jenny Eclair

Looking back, it's very clear to me that my father was a depressive – it was just never diagnosed... My mother had no patience with that kind of thing... She said to me: 'Judy, there's no such thing as depression. Your father was just miserable.'

Judy Finnigan

I did one session of therapy, but decided to manage it in my head. Therapy killed John Cleese's humour. Before therapy: 'Fawlty Towers'. Afterwards: books about dysfunctional families.

Ade Edmondson

To wear your heart on your sleeve isn't a very good plan; you should wear it inside, where it functions best.

Margaret Thatcher

I hardly ever worry. I don't suffer from depression, I don't even have moods – if you're in a bad mood, you're wasting time.

Jeremy Clarkson

Forget the psychiatry. Bottling It Up Is Best. Every time. So you die a little younger, what the hell? At least you get a bigger crowd at your funeral.

Maureen Lipman

Drugs and Addiction

I was innocent about drugs. The first time somebody said to me, at a party in London, 'Would you like some Charlie?' I said, 'No, thank you, I'm wearing Tweed by Lenthéric.'

Lily Savage, aka Paul O'Grady

There was a period with all the drugs and the fur coats... We went mad... I don't regret one single line, one night out. I think that's why people loved us from the start... given the circumstances, you'd do the fucking same.

Noel Gallagher

Taking LSD is like going to Stratford-on-Avon: you only need to go there once.

John Peel

I don't see the point of most drugs, especially Ecstasy. I think if I wanted to get dehydrated and jump around with a load of people I've never met, I could go to a Methodist barn dance.

Victoria Wood

Clubbers in Yorkshire have taken to using dental syringes to inject ecstasy directly into their mouths. This dangerous practice is known as E-by-gum.

Anon

I don't do drugs, but I did have a space cake once. I just heard the word 'cake'. I just found it really dry. I might not know drugs, but I do know cake. A bit of buttercream wouldn't have gone astray. It's almost like they hadn't thought about the 'cake' part at all.

Sarah Millican

Police are warning that teenagers in Yorkshire have been injecting themselves with curry powder to get high cheaply. Two are reported to be in a Korma.

Anon

Can you imagine walking through the Priory and seeing Robbie Williams coming over, say, in a fucking dressing gown? That's enough to drive anyone to heroin.

Noel Gallagher

If more people did WI, there'd be half the need for hallucinogenic drugs.

Chris Harper, Calendar Girls

He's been sniffing those dolly blues again!

Uncle Mort, I Didn't Know You Cared

Pub

Three milk stouts – and make sure there's no lipstick on the glasses!

Ena Sharples, Coronation Street

A good pub should smell like a mixture of the trenches and cheese and onion crisps – a smell you can chew on.

Jenny Eclair

I don't like these brewery-inspired female-friendly pubs – the kind of places where you can read a Virago classic and drink coffee all day. What's the point of that? If I want to drink and read at the same time, I'll take a can of Stella into the library like normal people.

Jenny Eclair

The thing about this place is that you can relax and switch off. And my mobile phone doesn't work.

Roger O'Neill (F), at the Old Silent Inn, high in the Pennine hills of West Yorkshire

I love them rough pubs. I went on quiz night, the first question was, 'Who are you looking at?' The prize was an alibi for a fortnight.

Mickey Finn

Rough? In my local, if you have two ears, you're overdressed.

Pete Collins

I wandered into a pub in Doncaster and commented to the barman how quaint it looked with sawdust all over the floor. 'Ah, that's not sawdust,' he said, 'that's last night's furniture.'

Paul Mills

As for the darts team, it is not true to say that there will be no welcome for them – they are valued customers of many years' standing. However, it is true to say that there will be no dartboard on the premises after the alterations.

Stockport Messenger

A fellow was in a pub that was just about to close, and was chatting to the barmaid, when in rushed a young fellow who gasped, 'Give me a beer, quick!' He drank it and paid for it, then ran up the side of the wall, across the ceiling, down the other side, and out. The other fellow looked at the barmaid and said, 'That's a peculiar chap.' 'Yes,' she said, 'he never said goodnight.'

Gracie Fields

This beer's not bad, if you disregard the taste. Shall we stop on for a couple more?

Uncle Mort, *Uncle Mort's North Country*

Alcohol

—What is your favourite drink?
—Alcohol.

Interviewer and Brian Clough

Want some coffee? I'd offer you a beer but I've only got six cans.

Terry Collier, *The Likely Lads*

A lot of men get very funny about women drinking: they don't really like it. Well, I'm sorry, lads, but if we didn't get pissed, most of you would never get a shag.

Jenny Eclair

—Do you drink in the morning?
—Of course I drink in the bloody morning. Presuming I know it is the morning.

Barrister and Anne Robinson, *Memoirs of an Unfit Mother*

We used to have a pint at every stop, and we used to have about ten stops in a day.

William Hague, on his days as a brewery driver's mate

Jilly Goolden was on characteristic form with a rose named after a wine...'You taste the wine and it tastes exactly how the rose would taste if you were to taste the rose.' Gertrude Stein used to say things like that. People crossed the road when they saw her coming.

Nancy Banks-Smith

Ugh! Too much tonic, Larkins. I've told you a thousand times, there's no malaria in this part of the world.

Lady Patience Hardacre, to her maid, *Brass*

Have you tried that Retsina? It's a Greek wine made of pine cones. It's just like disinfectant. It's brilliant. It means you can throw up and clean the toilet at the same time.

Jenny Eclair

Good Evenin', Ossifer: Drunk

I know what you're thinking: 'You've been drinking again, Paul.' No, well, yes, but I know when to stop. If I'm lying on my back, choking on my own vomit, I know I should only have one, maybe two, more drinks and after that I'd better stick to shorts.

Paul Calf, aka Steve Coogan

Three units is one large glass of wine, and for all the effect this has on a 16-stone man like me, I may as well suck the moisture from a clump of moss. I drink at least a bottle of wine a night. And before going to bed I have a small tumbler of vodka.

Jeremy Clarkson

I don't like being told what a safe drinking limit is. They just want us to stay in and eat turnips.

Mark E. Smith

When I do go out with Russell Brand, I sit and get progressively more pissed... I go to him, 'Just have a fucking beer! One beer!' And he says to me that if he has one beer he'll probably end up in a crack house in Kings Cross within forty minutes. I'm, like, 'Brilliant, I'll come with you!'

Noel Gallagher

He came out of the pub drunk the other night. There were two nuns walking towards him, and one went either side of him. He said, 'How the hell did she do that?'

Colin Crompton

Drunk as usual, he lay on a zebra crossing and cried, 'I'll play this ruddy piano if it kills me.'

Les Dawson

I found a nice drive out from Morecambe to a little country pub in a village miles from anywhere, up in the Lake District, with my mate, Tommy, the boozer. He said to the landlord, 'Have you got a big black dog with a white collar in this village?' The landlord said, 'No, we haven't.' He said, 'Well, have you got a big black cat with a white collar?' The landlord said, 'No, we haven't.' Tommy looked at me and said, 'There you are. It *was* the vicar I ran over.'

Colin Crompton

He went on one of those continental coach trips for his holidays. He was the only one on the bus who could see nothing wrong with the Tower of Pisa.

Colin Crompton

He supped so much on the boat coming back, they had to pay duty on him to get him back in the country.

Colin Crompton

I don't drink as a rule, not wishing to have a liver the size of a hot-water bottle. If I need a 'buzz', as I call it, I have a piccalilli sandwich with Worcester sauce; that takes your mind off your bunions, believe you me.

Kitty, *Victoria Wood, As Seen on TV*

Life would be so colourful if only I had a drink problem.

Morrissey

He's a very abstemious bloke – wears the tightest jockstrap this side of Chorlton-cum-Hardy.

Linda Preston, I Didn't Know You Cared

Smoking

Man, the creature who knows he must die, who has dreams larger than his destiny, who is forever working a confidence trick on himself, needs an ally... Mine has been tobacco.

J.B. Priestley

[*to Cyril Blamire*] If I had a match I could light me fag. [*Blamire gives him a match and he turns to Norman Clegg*] If I had a fag...

William 'Compo' Simmonite, Last of the Summer Wine

—I'm looking for French cigarettes. I don't suppose you have any?
—No, but we have English ones you can smoke with a foreign accent.

Customer and Arkwright, Open All Hours

—Cigarette, Vicar?
—Oh, thank you. I'm supposed to be stopping, but, then, on the other hand, it's hardly fitting for me to be seen trying to live forever, is it?

Norman Clegg and the Vicar, Last of the Summer Wine

I'm trying to give up two of my worst habits: smoking and masturbation. I'm finding it difficult as I'm a 20-a-day man. And I smoke like a chimney.

Paul Calf, aka Steve Coogan

Smokers: Enjoy seemingly longer holidays by stopping smoking on your first day off, making every day thereafter appear to be 72 hours long.

Top tip, *Viz* magazine

Tobacco gives you little pauses, a rest from life. I don't suppose anyone smoking a pipe would have road rage, would they?

David Hockney

Food is really just a prelude for smoking – a bit like sex. You have to go through the whole procedure just so you'll enjoy a fag more than you would if you hadn't done it.

Jeremy Clarkson

If I could change one law I would reverse the smoking ban immediately. I was in a pub last Saturday night, just having a quiet pint, and this fella gets his baby out and changes its nappy on the table next to me. That would have never happened before the smoking ban.

Mark E. Smith

—My grandad smoked 60 a day all his life from being 16. And he liked a pint. He never worried about it, he just got on with his life. He knew how to enjoy himself, that fella.
—He were a good laugh then were he?
—I don't know. I never knew him. He died when he was 32.

Joan Bell and Tanya, *Early Doors*

Age and Ageing

In an M&S food hall in Truro, two sales ladies walked past me. One nudged the other and asked me, 'Were you one of the Likely Lads on television?' 'Mmmmm,' I replied. The second one said: 'Oh, I thought so. That ages me, doesn't it?' Sigh.

Rodney Bewes

A man has to realise he's not as young as he used to be. In the autumn of his life, there are signs and portents that tell him: you get out of breath playing chess... your wedding suit comes back into fashion... you wake up one morning and find you've got a bald-headed son...

Ken Dodd

An acquaintance this afternoon said, 'How are you, Mr Priestley?' I replied as usual, 'Old and fat.' 'You said that the last time I asked you,' he declared. 'Well, there you are,' I told him. 'Now, I'm old, fat *and* repetitive.'

J.B. Priestley

—Do you feel old?
—I feel like a kebab with onions on.

Interviewer and Paul Gascoigne

I don't know how old she is, but she doesn't look her age.

Thora Hird, on Dora Bryan

At that awkward age between birth and death.

Roger McGough

You still chase after girls – but you can't remember why. And your wife doesn't mind you chasing after girls because, as she says, 'Our dog chases after cars, and he can't drive.'

Ken Dodd

When I was young I used to worry about screwing; now I worry about unscrewing.

Jilly Cooper, on wrestling with hard-to-open jar-lids

The problem with old age is it creeps up on you – like a ninja. You think, 'Ooh, I'm really young,' and then one day you catch yourself tucking your shirt into your underpants – this is really comfortable. Before you know it, you're unplugging the telly at the end of the night and sucking barley sugars on a coach-trip to Ely Cathedral and realising the only thing you've got to look forward to in your day is hearing the words, 'Cashier number 4, please!'

Jeff Green

I never used to worry about body hair when I was younger... Now it's all over the shop!... Apparently, these days, it has to go into a shape. You can't do what I do and just chop the odd chunk off with the nail scissors.

Victoria Wood

I found my first grey pubic hair the other day. It was in a kebab, but there you go.

Jeff Green

If my boobs got any lower, I would have to buy them their own pair of shoes.

Jeanette Winterson

In about five years' time I shall be carrying a very big brolly and shall be a very cross old bag and hitting people if I don't like the way they treat me.

Diana Rigg, aged 70

One of the delights known to age and beyond the grasp of youth is that of Not Going.

J.B. Priestley

He's not deaf. It's totally selective. He can hear a bag of oven chips being opened from three doors away.

Dolly, *Dinnerladies*

I think the main reason we all fear the flowing sands of time is that perhaps it reminds us that one day we will visit the dark place from whence no one returns. No, not Rhyl – the other place...

Jeff Green

The greatest fear about old age is the fear that it may go on too long.

A.J.P. Taylor

When Jeremy comes to see me, the first thing he does is pat the cushions on my settee. 'It's OK, Mother,' he shouts, 'you've not started wetting them yet!' We have this agreement. Whenever I start dribbling my food or having accidents on the settee, he'll drive me up to Beachy Head and push me over the edge. It's a mutual agreement.

Shirley Clarkson

Holding Back The Years

Good morning, madam. May I interest you in our skin-care range... We do sell this astringent – I don't know if it's strong enough for what you need, but it brought my chip pan up lovely.

Department Store Assistant, *Victoria Wood, As Seen on TV*

You know Ethel Higginbottom? She's 'ad 'er face lifted. It's not safe to leave anything lying about these days, is it?

Fanny Fairbottom, aka Norman Evans, *Over the Garden Wall*

I have had me eyes done. I looked tired because I were up arf t'night worrying about me wrinkles.

Jane McDonald, *Loose Women*

—I had a mole removed.
—Where?
—Just south of Manchester.
—I meant where on your body?
—So did I.

Daphne Moon and Niles Crane (F), *Frasier*

Oh, God, spare me! Why can't I just grow old gracefully – like Peter Stringfellow?

Jeff Green

I am going to carry on colouring my hair, wearing diamonds and painting my nails until the day I die.

Jenni Murray

I'm looking forward to certain elements of my physical decay... First thing I'm gonna do, when I get my Freedom Bus Pass, is take ten minutes to get on the bus... and, yes , I actually want a bath with a door in it... And finally, that seat in the chemist will be mine!

Jeff Green

Popping Yer Clogs: Death

Old Harry is on his death bed, but perks up when he smells something good cooking downstairs. He sniffs the air and realises it's boiled ham. He calls down to his wife, 'Hey, pet, I could eat a couple of slices of that ham you're cooking.' 'Don't be daft,' his wife shouts back, 'that's for the funeral tea.'

Geordie joke

—I wish I was skiing.
—Do you ski, Mr Laurel?
—No, but I would still rather be skiing than doing this.

Stan Laurel, on his deathbed, and Nurse

He's too old for euthanasia. He hasn't got the constitution for it.

Annie Brandon, *I Didn't Know You Cared*

I'm not scared of dying. I've already had three near-death experiences. That last one, there was a bright light at the end of a long, white passage, and Dusty Springfield was beckoning to me, with a lovely smile. Turned out I'd passed out in the Mersey Tunnel with a drag act.

Petula, *Dinnerladies*

As a boy, I was once nearly run down by an articulated lorry that carried the slogan 'Have a break, have a Kit Kat', and it occurred to me that, as a northern death, it could not compare with being lost in a trawler off Hull, or buried under a collapsed coal face.

Andrew Martin

For a true Northerner it's a fate worse than death, dying in the South.

Uncle Mort, *Uncle Mort's South Country*

I can't see me just going out in my sleep. I think I'd probably stand up and punch the doctor before I went.

Carla Lane

I don't want to die peacefully in my sleep. I'd rather choke to death. On Johnny Depp.

Jenny Eclair

If I 'ad my way, I'd just like to go like me mother did: she just sat up, broke wind and died.

Ena Sharples, *Coronation Street*

A dying wife says to her husband, 'When I go, I want you to marry again.' He replies, 'Oh, pet, don't be saying things like that.' 'But I want you to be happy,' she says. 'How could I be happy without you, dear?' says he. 'And I don't want my wardrobe to go to waste,' she adds. 'I want you to give her all my nice clothes.' 'Oh,' says her husband, 'I don't think they'll fit her.'

Geordie joke

Popping Yer Clogs: Death

Will you make sure I'm buried in the family vaults, pointing toward
Blackpool. Me grandad won the vaults in a raffle of the bankrupt stock of
a monumental mason who ran off with a lady yodeller from Glossop.

Auntie Lil, *I Didn't Know You Cared*

I went round me grandma's flat. I walked in, she said: 'Guess who's dead?'
She wants me to guess! Where d'you start with something like that? 'Connie,'
she says, 'from the flat upstairs. I heard a thud during "Bargain Hunt."'

Peter Kay

—Gone at last!
—No, I bloody 'aven't! You'll know when I'm going. I'll take me teeth out.
—You'll what? It's the kitchen for you, then. You're not being laid out in
the parlour with no teeth.
—I am. They're promised to old Bert Taylor.
—What's he going to do with 'em?
—What the 'ell d'you think he's going to do with 'em? There's years in
these yet.

Nelly and Joshua Pledge, *Nearest and Dearest*

My husband's dead. It's very upsetting... I keep finding things of his around
the house. I found his favourite mug the other day. It's chipped and cracked
and very old, but he loved that mug. He said he'd never be able to find
another one like it – 'Man City, League Champions' it said on the side.

Pauline Calf, aka Steve Coogan

The best thing to do, when you've got a dead body and it's your husband's
on the kitchen floor and you don't know what to do about it, is to make
yourself a strong cup of tea.

Anthony Burgess

I don't want a cup of tea. I'll have a gin. Save on the electric.

Bev Unwin, Coronation Street

—Did you know Nancy Wilson's husband had died?
—No! Was it anything serious?

Alice and Sadie, Live Theatre

How's his widow bearing up? I always knew she drew great strength from the fact that there was a better life to come – with him from Albion Street.

Mrs Blewitt, Open All Hours

—What happened when he, er, you know...
—He'd just gone into the back garden to pick a cabbage for Sunday dinner. He bent down, keeled over and that was it.
—Oh, how awful – so sudden, like. What did you do?
—I had to open a tin of peas.

Bereaved Wife and Friend

A friend of mine died of dyslexia. He choked on his own Vimto.

Dave Spikey

My father died of natural causes. That were the whole trouble. He'd never suffered from natural causes before, so once he'd caught it he'd got no immunity.

Uncle Mort, I Didn't Know You Cared

—He dropped dead in the middle of Matalan! They split his ashes... His sister, who's living here, took half, and his other sister, who lives in America, took the other half. He'd never been out of Manchester in his life and now, half of him is in Salford and the other half of him is in San Francisco.
—Which half?

Mary and Nana, The Royle Family

My aunt's funeral was in the crematorium. She wanted to be buried but she doesn't know to this day that she's been cremated.

Mary Boucher, overheard

[*paying her respects*] —I'll say this, pet, your Ernie looks happy laid out there.
—Well, he died in his sleep, so he doesn't know he's dead yet.

Mourner and Wife of Deceased, Geordie joke

Me granny died. She was 93, she sat in the chair, closed her eyes, went to sleep and never woke up again, which is nice, isn't it? The dentist shit himself, obviously.

Dave Spikey

My grandmother died of hypothermia. It had nothing to do with the weather. She'd been shoplifting in Bejam's.

Lily Savage, aka Paul O'Grady

That's what the North was like in them days. People were always dying. It were a fact of life, were death. People snuffed it as regular as clockwork. They didn't complain and moan about it. They just got on with the job. Not like now. They make a real bloody song and dance about it. It's reached epidemic proportions in the North now – not wanting to die.

Uncle Mort, Uncle Mort's North Country

My father died at 83. It was by far the highest score he ever made.

Chris Thomas, on his father, Tony, a cricketer

My agent died at ninety. I always think he was a hundred and kept ten per cent for himself.

Ken Dodd

Thora Hird only once played in Shakespeare – the nurse in 'Romeo and Juliet', and she could never have thought to play Cleopatra. But Charmian's lament for the dead Cleopatra is a proper epitaph for this droll-faced Northern girl who, in the course of a long and happy life, took her place among the best that we have: 'Now boast thee, Death, in thy possession lies a lass unparallel'd.'

Alan Bennett

Tell you what, though, I'd give all the bloody money in the world to 'ave one more bloody row with 'er.

Jim Royle, on the death of Nana, *The Royle Family*

Then T'worms'll Come An' Eat Thee Up: **Funeral**

—So, you're going to Parslow's funeral.
—Yes, even though it's very unlikely he'll ever go to mine.

Mrs Blewitt and Arkwright, *Open All Hours*

A wife on her deathbed says to her husband: 'I want you, as my dying wish, to travel in the first car with my mother.' Her husband replies: 'Just to please you, pet, I will, but I'm telling you now, it'll spoil me day.'

Geordie joke

She's gone over to Rawtenstall to bury her father. She took t'family dentures with 'er; there was talk of a boiled 'am send-off, see.

George Fairchild, *Brass*

In India, if a man dies, the widow flings herself onto the funeral pyre. If a man dies in this country, the woman just drags herself into the kitchen and says, 'Seventy-two baps, Connie, you slice, I'll spread.'

Victoria Wood

—Shall you have boiled ham at the funeral tea, or are you a devotee of brawn?
—I never give a funeral tea. I tell folks to bring their own sandwiches and bottles of drink. I don't charge very much for corkage.

Annie Brandon and Mrs Macclesfield, *I Didn't Know You Cared*

I'm wearing black cos I'm in mourning. And it makes me look slim.

Pauline Calf, aka Steve Coogan

[*trying on sunglasses to wear to a funeral*] It's a fine line between Jackie Onassis and Roy Orbison.

Blanche Hunt, *Coronation Street*

—I'm not getting rid of this suit. It keeps coming back into fashion.
—I bet Parslow's wearing a better suit than that and he's going to be cremated.

Arkwright and Nurse Gladys Emmanuel, *Open All Hours*

In 'Coronation Street', Mrs Duckworth had a grand send-off. The wreath spelled 'Vera'. 'Veronica' was dearer.

Nancy Banks-Smith

A rude wreath at Jimmy Butterfield's funeral in Newcastle summed up his laugh-a-minute approach to life. The six-foot floral tribute of red and white carnations spelled out his favourite swear word. Jimmy's daughter, Sue, admitted, 'It was a bit awkward going to the florist to ask for Dad's wreath. The girl couldn't spell the word.'

The Sun (the wreath spelt: 'BOLLOCKS')

I thought that Potters of Johnson Street would have done the interment because they put our Jack down last year and we've 'ad no trouble since. So 'elp me God, the Co-op buried him! Cheap, cheap, cheap! Anything for the divi, that's them.

Ada Shufflebottom, aka Les Dawson

A DIY MDF coffin? You won't catch me goin' to meet my maker in a flat-pack.

Blanche Hunt, *Coronation Street*

[*Uncle Mort throws a handful of dirt onto the coffin of his deceased wife*]
—What are you thinking of, Mort? Memories of your poor dead wife, Edna?
—No, I was just thinking what a champion crop of onions you could grow on this soil.

Annie Brandon and Uncle Mort, *I Didn't Know You Cared*

It is a fact that, up north, cemeteries are a way of life. The family grave inspires the same mixture of tenderness and irritation as the family allotment. Both need weeding.

Jeanette Winterson

Only t'other day I went to a funeral. I was coming away from t'graveside, a chap looked at me and says, 'How old are you?' I said, 'I'm 82.' He said, 'I don't think it's much use thee goin' 'ome at all.'

Frank Randle

My grandmother died, and after the funeral, recovering from the innate vulgarity of the cremation service when the gramophone record stuck on 'Abi-abi-abi-abi-de with me', the whole family trooped home and discovered some crates of Australian burgundy under the stairs. A rip-roaring party ensued and soon a lower middle busybody who lived next door came bustling over to see if anything was wrong. Whereupon my father-in-law, holding a glass and seeing her coming up the path, uttered the immortal line: 'Who is this intruding on our grief?'

Jilly Cooper

Funerals and weddings are all the same in our house. It's just one less drunk.

Lily Savage, aka Paul O'Grady

In Loving Memory: Epitaphs and Obituaries

An old Yorkshireman's wife dies. As she was a God-fearing Christian and regular church-goer, he orders a headstone for her with the words: 'She was thine.' Unfortunately, when he goes to collect the stone, it says: 'She was thin.' 'What about the 'e'?' he complains. The stonemason promises to correct it. Next day he goes back to collect the stone, to find that it now says: 'Ee, she was thin.'

Old Yorkshire joke

If I died tomorrow, you know what I'd have carved on my gravestone: 'None the bloody wiser.'

Terry Collier, *Whatever Happened to the Likely Lads?*

—How do you want to be remembered?
—As Manchester's answer to the H-bomb.

Interviewer and Morrissey

I couldn't care less what anyone writes in my obituary. In fact I know it will be 'Man who asked same question 14 times dies'.

Jeremy Paxman, on his interview with Michael Howard (F)

I never said I was deep.

Jarvis Cocker, anticipating a shallow grave

Teenage dreams so hard to beat.

Words on John Peel's gravestone, from the lyrics of his favourite song,
'Teenage Kicks' by The Undertones

When Alan Bennett dies (a long time hence, one trusts) England should raise a statue. Outside Mornington Crescent Tube station: in calcified Yorkshire pud, perhaps – glaring angrily, through those famous horn-rims and quiff, at every passing bendy bus.

John Sutherland (F)

Eddie Paynter, the Lancashire and England batsman, provided the perfect epitaph for Wally Hammond. He was asked for his abiding memory of the great man. He had witnessed Hammond's majesty in its prime and at close quarters. But Paynter was from Oswaldtwistle and spoke plain. 'Wally,' said Eddie, thinking hard, 'he liked a shag.'

Michael Parkinson

Lashes to lashes, bust to bust...

Epitaph for the Flat Slags, Mark Shipley

Here's to the Iron Lady – may she rust in peace.

Epitaph suggested for Mrs Thatcher

Heaven and Hell

When I get to heaven I shall produce on my behalf, in hope of salvation after all, my stock of failures and frustrations; my attempts to become a leader writer on the 'Manchester Guardian', my attempts to sing the Abschied of Wotan; my attempts to understand Hegel; my attempts to spin a fast ball from the leg to the off stump.

Neville Cardus

I'd like to believe in heaven, not least because I'd like to meet my mum and dad again. I'd like to know whether the Welsh dresser was meant to go to me or my brother, really.

John Peel

My mother was worried about whether my father would be wearing pyjamas or a mackintosh in the afterlife.

George Melly

—You're certain it's 'Men Only' up there, and they don't 'ave rugby league and Eddie Waring?
—No, what they've got up there is sheepdog trials, open-top trams, spittoons, and all the pubs 'ave beer from the wood.
—Aye, I bet they're closed on bloody Sundays through.

Uncle Mort and Carter Brandon, *I Didn't Know You Cared*

I'm going to hell not heaven. I mean, the Devil's got all the good gear. What's God got? The Inspiral Carpets and nuns.

> Liam Gallagher

To different minds, the same world is a hell, and a heaven.

> J.B. Priestley

Ee By Gum, Lord: Religion

That's a very deep theological question you've asked. I'll have to think about this: 'If the twelve disciples had a football team, who would I leave on the bench?'

> Vicar, to Andy Capp

Russell Brand's a big posh Essex boy former junkie who's been to the dark side and got into Hare Krishna. He's never seen a council estate. I'm a gruff Northerner who drinks Red Stripe. He finds that fascinating. He's all, 'But Noel darling, don't you believe in a higher existence?' and I'm like, 'Not dressed in a sheet banging a tambourine, you big jessie.'

> Noel Gallagher

—How many Protestants does it take to put in a lightbulb?
—None. They live in eternal darkness.

> Sister Mary Immaculate, aka Caroline Aherne

I'm not a religious woman, but I find if you say no to everything you can hardly tell the difference.

> Mrs Featherstone, *Open All Hours*

It's 'Bringing in the Sheaves' not 'Bringing in the Sheaths', yer daft trollope.

Lily Savage, aka Paul O'Grady

God

—No daughter of mine's being married in any church other than the Church of England.
—I don't see what difference it makes. I mean, there are many roads to God.
—There may be many roads, but I've always considered the Church of England to be the M1.

Mrs Chambers and Bob Ferris, Whatever Happened to the Likely Lads?

—Is God alive?
—I'm far too provincial to answer that question.

Interviewer and Morrissey, Rolling Stone magazine

It all boils down to either you believe or you don't. And I don't believe there's a God who says, 'If you drink, do drugs and swear and rob houses, you're not sitting on my cloud.'

Noel Gallagher

Hopes are to be dashed, expectations not to be realised, because that's the way God, who speaks with a southern accent, has arranged things.

Alan Bennett

God was so tattooed on to me that I can't but believe in him.

Jeanette Winterson

God – a likeness.

Inscription on a picture of Liverpool player, Kenny Dalglish,
hung by John Peel in his office

In the new form of service God is throughout referred to as You; only one Thou left in the world, and the fools have abolished it. Of course they can't do away with the vocative, which is every bit as archaic, so we still say 'O God'. It's a good job God doesn't have a name, or we'd probably be calling him Dave.

Alan Bennett, Writing Home

Trust in the Lord – and keep your bowels open.

Doris Humphrey, advice from her father

The Clergy

I asked why he was a priest, and he said if you have to work for anybody an absentee boss is best.

Jeanette Winterson, The Passion

I remember as I came down from the pulpit after my first few sermons being disappointed that the world hadn't changed.

Dr Michael Turnbull, Bishop of Durham

—Then I had to get my skates on for Evensong.
—Evensong on ice? The Church must be desperate.

Canon Throbbing and Arthur Wicksteed, Habeas Corpus

Go and ask the vicar what's happened to my glass of communion wine. If he hasn't poured it out yet, tell him I don't want that rubbish he had on Sunday. It was very tart, was that. Barely worth turning up for. Then they wonder why attendances are falling off, serving up muck like that.

Count Arthur Strong, aka Steve Delaney

My wife was admitted to hospital for an operation, and I drove her there. The nurse wrote down all her details and said: 'Religion?' My wife said, 'None,' and the nurse wrote down, 'Nun.' I said to her, 'Nun? You just put *me* down as next of kin!' She said, 'Oh, I thought they might have changed the rules.'

Dave Spikey

—What is your nationality?
—Church of England.

Nurse and Paul Gascoigne, before an operation

Life, the Universe and Everything Else

Life

—It's been some week, Andy. First, the wife leaves me and then my dog dies.
—That's life for you, Walter. Just when you're on a high, something comes along to knock you down.

Walter and Andy Capp

I don't blame anyone for bringing me into the world, but I do feel that life is excessively overrated.

Morrissey

In the chocolate box of life, the top layer's already gone, and someone's pinched the orange creme from the bottom.

Bob Ferris, *The Likely Lads*

—Life's not worth living, is it?
—Aye, I wish there was summat else y'could do wi' it.

Les Brandon and Uncle Mort, *I Didn't Know You Cared*

You've got your whole life ahead of you. You're just at the dawn of your disasters.

Terry Collier, *Whatever Happened to the Likely Lads?*

Life is what happens to you while you're busy making other plans.

John Lennon

Life is a wretched grey Saturday, but it has to be lived through.

Anthony Burgess

We have to go through life with the air of quiet expectancy which belongs to the motorist parked on a double yellow line.

Roy Clarke

—As well as working as a stand-up, you do Radio 4's 'Just a Minute', have been a captain on BBC1's 'Have I got News For You' and you have had your own radio show. Can life get any better?
—Yes, I could grow little hands just above my hips. Think of the money you could save on belts.

Interviewer and Ross Noble

Think On! Philosophy

I've been doing some blue cheese thinking...

Count Arthur Strong, aka Steve Delaney

My greatest strength, I think, is that come what may I somehow cope.

Margaret Thatcher

Two things in life have served me well. One is an in-built shit detector. And the other is a belief in keeping the channels clear, by which I mean remaining open to change, to new people or ideas, and to the possibility that I might just be wrong.

Maureen Lipman

In a nutshell, my philosophy is this: Never stop paying attention to things. Never make your mind up finally. Do not hold beliefs.

A.S. Byatt

I don't like being on my own because you think a lot and I don't like to think a lot.

Paul Gascoigne

Owner of a Shed. And a Son. Thinks the World is Wonky.

Alun Cochrane, title of Edinburgh show

Thinking can ruin your health which is why, of course, people turn to politics instead.

Norman Clegg, *Last of the Summer Wine*

I'm contemplating thinking about thinking...but...it's overrated. Just get another drink in!

Robbie Williams

Don't let the bastards grind you down!

Arthur Seaton, *Saturday Night and Sunday Morning*

Who Are You?

I am what I am.

Margaret Thatcher

I'm always me – the man who says the right thing at the wrong time.

Brian Clough

Whatever people say I am, that's what I'm not because they don't know a bloody thing about me! God knows what I am.

Arthur Seaton, *Saturday Night and Sunday Morning*

Be yourself is about the worst advice you can give to some people.

J.B. Priestley

Not only don't I know who I am, but I'm very suspicious of people who do know who they are. I am sometimes ten or twelve people a day, and sometimes four or five people an hour.

Tom Baker

It's not weird, is it? I want to come in as Heidi tomorrow.

Robbie Williams, *Somebody Someday*

I can only simply be me, which is a full-time occupation and causes terrible backache.

Morrissey

Perhaps the rare and simple pleasure of being seen for what one is compensates for the misery of being it.

Margaret Drabble

In My Day: The Past

Three elderly men were walking across the dales chatting idly. 'Do you know, I can remember right back to my christening,' said the first. 'I were all dressed up in t'robe and taken to this church where t'vicar splashed water on me.' 'Aye, so can I,' said the second. 'But that's nowt. I remember being in t'womb. It were lovely and warm, then I were squeezed through this right tiny hole into bright daylight.' 'And so can I,' replied the third. 'But that's nowt either. I remember going on a picnic on t'Dales with me dad – and coming back with me mam.'

Bill Shipton

It's the only thing to look forward to – the past.

Ian La Frenais and Mike Hugg (F), signature tune, *Whatever Happened to the Likely Lads?*

I'll never forget them days in the 1930s. Bert and I 'ad nothing – no food, no carpets, no furniture. And then came the Depression.

Ada Shufflebottom, aka Les Dawson

—Eh, you were lucky to have a room! We used to have to live in t'corridor!

—Oh, we used to dream of livin' in a corridor! Would ha' been a palace to us. We used to live in an old water tank on a rubbish tip.

Two Yorkshiremen, *At Last, The 1948 Show*

Them were the days. If you had three jam-jars, you had half a tea-set.

Billy Martin

—Oh, we never had a cup. We used to have to drink out of a rolled up newspaper.

—The best we could manage was to suck on a piece of damp cloth.

Two Yorkshiremen, *At Last, The 1948 Show*

And no one had cars. If you wanted to get run over, you'd to catch a bus to the main road.

Old Bag, *Victoria Wood, As Seen on TV*

You were lucky. We lived for three months in a paper bag in a septic tank. We used to have to get up at six in the morning, clean the paper bag, eat a crust of stale bread, go to work down t'mill, fourteen hours a day, week-in week-out, for sixpence a week, and when we got home our Dad would thrash us to sleep wi' his belt.

Yorkshireman, *At Last, The 1948 Show*

And we didn't do all this keep-fit. We got our exercise lowering coffins out of upstairs windows. In fact, if people were very heavy we used to ask them to die downstairs.

Old Bag, *Victoria Wood, As Seen on TV*

They don't know they're born. At his age, I never had a best shirt. People used to live two or three to a shirt in them days.

Arkwright, *Open All Hours*

Well, of course, we had it tough. We used to 'ave to get up out of shoebox at twelve o'clock at night and lick road clean wi' t' tongue. We had two bits of cold gravel, worked 24 hours a day at mill for sixpence every four years, and when we got home our Dad would slice us in two wi' t' bread knife.

Yorkshireman, *At Last, The 1948 Show*

And we weren't having hysterectomies every two minutes either, like the girls these days. If something went wrong down below, you kept your gob shut and turned up the wireless.

Old Bag, *Victoria Wood, As Seen on TV*

Right. I had to get up in the morning at ten o'clock at night half an hour before I went to bed, drink a cup of sulphuric acid, work 29 hours a day down mill, and pay mill owner for permission to come to work, and when we got home, our Dad and our mother would kill us and dance about on our graves singing Hallelujah.

Yorkshireman, *At Last, The 1948 Show*

—I sure feel sorry for the kids of today.
—Yeah, what will they be able to tell *their* kids they 'ad to do without?

Flo and Andy Capp

—I wish I were young again!
— Yeah, rickets, T.B. and rationing – those were the days!

Emily Bishop and Blanche Hunt, *Coronation Street*

The Future

—A hundred years from now, everyone'll be run by computers...
—Aye, Carter, the rest of England'll be like you describe it...but not the
North... I've got faith in the old and tried values of the North of England.
We'll never give in. Come 2084...the North will be alive and kicking, with
rampant gloom and despondency and the ultimate accolade of all –
cricket played once more at Bramall Lane.

Carter Brandon and Uncle Mort, Uncle Mort's North Country

Index

italic page numbers indicate references to, rather than quotations by, the subject of the index entry

Index

Index

Index